How Students Come to Be, Know, and Do

Studies of learning are too frequently conceptualized only in terms of knowledge development. Yet it is vital to pay close attention to the social and emotional aspects of learning in order to understand why and how it occurs. *How Students Come to Be, Know, and Do* builds a theoretical argument for and a methodological approach to studying learning in a holistic way. The authors provide examples of urban fourth graders from diverse cultural and linguistic backgrounds studying science as a way to illustrate how this model contributes to a more complete and complex understanding of learning in school settings. What makes this book unique is its insistence that to fully understand human learning we have to consider the affective volitional processes of learning along with the more familiar emphasis on knowledge and skills. Developing interest, persisting in the face of difficulty, actively listening to others' ideas, accepting and responding to feedback, and challenging ideas are crucial dimensions of students' experiences that are often ignored.

Leslie Rupert Herrenkohl, Ph.D., is Associate Professor in the Learning Sciences and Human Development and Cognition Programs in the College of Education at the University of Washington. She also teaches in the Elementary Master's in Teaching Program. Dr. Herrenkohl studies the intellectual, social, and emotional aspects of children's development as science learners in formal and informal settings. She enjoys collaborating with practitioners to apply developmental theory to support the design of learning environments. Her work has been included in the national panel summary of school-based science learning, *Taking Science to School: Learning and Teaching Science in Grades K–8* (2007) and was featured as one of twelve case examples in the volume on applying science research to teaching practice, *Ready, Set, Science! Putting Research to Work in K–8 Science Classrooms* (2008). She served on the oversight panel for the recently released *Surrounded by Science: Learning Science in Informal Environments* (2010). Dr. Herrenkohl has received funding from the National Science Foundation, the Spencer Foundation, and the James S. McDonnell Foundation.

Véronique Mertl is a doctoral candidate in human development and cognition in the College of Education at the University of Washington. Her research explores the social, affective, and contextual elements that influence learning, with a particular focus on collaboration and belongingness in and out of school. She currently studies professional and adolescent musicians. She seeks to understand musicians' interactions, networks, and trajectories, particularly how out-of-school art and music settings engage and empower youth. Mertl works as a researcher for the Learning in Informal and Formal Environments (LIFE) Center, a National Science Foundation Science of Learning Center. She is also a consultant for several music and arts organizations in the United States.

LEARNING IN DOING: SOCIAL, COGNITIVE,
AND COMPUTATIONAL PERSPECTIVES

SERIES EDITOR EMERITUS
John Seely Brown, *Xerox Palo Alto Research Center*

GENERAL EDITORS
Roy Pea, *Professor of Education and the Learning Sciences and Director, Stanford Center for Innovations in Learning, Stanford University*

Christian Heath, *The Management Centre, King's College, London*

Lucy A. Suchman, *Centre for Science Studies and Department of Sociology, Lancaster University, UK*

(Continued after the index)

How Students Come to Be, Know, and Do

A Case for a Broad View of Learning

LESLIE RUPERT HERRENKOHL

University of Washington

VÉRONIQUE MERTL

University of Washington

CAMBRIDGE
UNIVERSITY PRESS

KH

CAMBRIDGE UNIVERSITY PRESS
Cambridge, New York, Melbourne, Madrid, Cape Town, Singapore,
São Paulo, Delhi, Dubai, Tokyo, Mexico City

Cambridge University Press
32 Avenue of the Americas, New York, NY 10013-2473, USA

www.cambridge.org
Information on this title: www.cambridge.org/9780521515658

First published 2010

Printed in the United States of America

A catalog record for this publication is available from the British Library.

Library of Congress Cataloguing in Publication data

Herrenkohl, Leslie Rupert, 1966–
How students come to be, know, and do : a case for a broad view of learning / Leslie
Rupert Herrenkohl, Véronique Mertl.
   p.   cm.
Includes bibliographical references and index
ISBN 978-0-521-51565-8 Hardback
1. Learning – United States – Case studies.   2. Science – Study and teaching
(Elementary) – United States – Case studies.   3. Interpersonal relations – Study
and teaching (Elementary) – United States – Case studies.   4. Group work in
education – United States – Case studies.   5. City children – Education
(Elementary) – United States – Case studies.   I. Mertl, Véronique, 1972–
II. Title.   III. Series.
LB1060.H47   2010
370.15′230973 – dc22   2010018292

ISBN 978-0-521-51565-8 Hardback

Epigraph in chapter 4 reprinted by permission of the publisher from *On knowing:
Essays for the left hand* by Jerome Bruner, p. 116, Cambridge, Mass.: The Belknap
Press of Harvard University Press, Copyright © 1962, 1979 by the President and
Fellows of Harvard College.

9/9/11

To Mrs. Glenda and her students
To Madeline and Isaac

Contents

Series Foreword

This series for Cambridge University Press is widely known as an international forum for studies of situated learning and cognition. Innovative contributions are being made by anthropology; by cognitive, developmental, and cultural psychology; by computer science; by education; and by social theory. These contributions are providing the basis for new ways of understanding the social, historical, and contextual nature of learning, thinking, and practice that emerges from human activity. The empirical settings of these research inquiries range from the classroom to the workplace, to the high-technology office, and to learning in the streets and in other communities of practice. The situated nature of learning and remembering through activity is a central fact. It may appear obvious that human minds develop in social situations and extend their sphere of activity and communicative competencies. But cognitive theories of knowledge representation and learning alone have not provided sufficient insight into these relationships. This series was born of the conviction that new exciting interdisciplinary syntheses are underway as scholars and practitioners from diverse fields seek to develop theory and empirical investigations adequate for characterizing the complex relations of social and mental life, and for understanding successful learning wherever it occurs. The series invites contributions that advance our understanding of these seminal issues.

Roy Pea
Christian Heath
Lucy A. Suchman

Acknowledgments

This book has been in the making for a very long time. It is the result of 15 years of struggle with a nagging feeling that there was something missing from my accounts of science learning. My early attempts to articulate what I thought was missing, what I initially discussed as the role of self in subject matter learning, began while in graduate school. At that time, I was not particularly successful at communicating my ideas. The theoretical language and methodological tools I was trying to use did not do the job very well. So I initially took the safer path of discussing the cognitive and social aspects of how children learn to think like scientists. This work has been generative and provided me with a deep appreciation for how learning is a general as well as domain-specific social endeavor. It has also allowed me to experience firsthand the brilliant capabilities of all children. My work has been conducted in urban settings with diverse groups of students and has opened my eyes to the dangers of deficit models of schooling. I have been convinced that all students are resourceful and eager learners. The task for adults is to entice students to join the discussion and throw themselves wholeheartedly into learning so that they draw on and develop their knowledge, skills, and sense of themselves as science learners. This is risky social and personal business that engages intellectual as well as emotional demands. I've had the pleasure of watching some very capable teachers create these kinds of dynamic classroom environments with their students. However, as I continued to conduct research with different teacher-research partners in different states, the same nagging feeling that something was missing in my written accounts of learning kept coming up. I knew that I was not really capturing the whole story about how students learn science in classrooms with the amazing and dedicated teachers with whom I have worked. This book is an answer to my own persistent question: What's missing in my account of science learning?

There are many people who have helped me along this path. I owe a huge debt of gratitude to my first two mentors, Jim Wertsch and Annemarie Palincsar. Without them, it is fair to say, I would not be the person or thinker that I am today. I am deeply grateful for their support and the hours they dedicated to my learning and development as a young scholar. They were excellent role models of mentoring that I strive to live up to with my own students.

I am grateful for the support and generosity of time and talent from good friends and colleagues. When I first arrived at the University of Washington, my colleagues Pam Grossman, Deborah McCutchen, and Sam Wineburg were instrumental in encouraging and supporting my desire to understand learning from this broad view. I benefited from their generosity of time and spirit to review and provide feedback on my ideas and my writing. Jim Greeno and his students Melissa Gresalfi, Vicki Hand, and Randi Engle were partners in dialogue during early phases of this work. UW colleagues Elham Kazemi and Elizabeth Dutro and Clark graduate student colleagues Kevin O'Connor and Bill Penuel provided comments on drafts of this work that really helped push my thinking and improve my writing. I also benefited from hours of discussion with Eli Gottlieb when he was a postdoctoral Fellow at UW. UW College of Education Dean Pat Wasley supported my work at a time when I needed to focus solely on writing the manuscript. I am grateful to students who joined in my doctoral seminars over the years to discuss self and subject matter and what I now call a broad view of learning. In particular I'd like to thank Laura Adriance, Lindsay Cornelius, Sue Feldman, Brenda Hood, Sasha Lotas, Sandra Toro Martell, David Spring, Tammy Tasker, Kersti Tyson, Scott Votaw, and Sherry Yeary.

I am thankful for my collaborations with teachers who have tethered my theoretical flights of fancy to real-world educational contexts. I count my collaborations with teachers as one of the most rewarding aspects of my professional work. Thanks are due to Lezlie DeWater, Patty Jacobs, Keiko Kawasaki, Caryn

McCrohon, Maureen Reddy, and others whose names must remain confidential.

Grant support from a National Academy of Education/Spencer Postdoctoral Fellowship in 2000 provided time for initial sustained thinking about this broad view of learning. I am grateful for this support that allowed me to develop early versions of the Rich case that began to help me to get a toehold into what was missing in my accounts of learning. Without that fellowship year, this work would not have been launched. Over the years I also have received support from the James S. McDonnell Foundation and the National Science Foundation that has furthered my understanding of science learning and teaching in ways that helped me more fully articulate my broad view of learning. However, I take sole responsibility, together with Véronique Mertl, for the statements that are made and the views that are expressed in this book.

A special thank you is due to my doctoral student, Véronique Mertl, who joined me in the process of analyzing data and writing the book. I am continually impressed by Véronique's analytic eye and the insight she brings to conversational interaction. Writing the book would have been a lonely experience without her company along the way. I appreciated her effort throughout this process and look forward to a bright and shining future ahead for her!

To Leslie Rupert Herrenkohl, I, Véronique, extend sincere thanks and gratitude for inviting me to collaborate on this book. I appreciate Leslie's thoughtful reflection and our many dynamic dialogues around learning, youth, and research. This exceptional opportunity has profoundly challenged my thinking and understanding about how people develop and learn. As an advisor and a mentor, Leslie has guided me with both knowledge and care. I thank her for inspiring me to pursue my interests and to grow as a scholar and researcher.

This book was originally planned as a series of papers. Véronique and I owe Ellice Forman a thank you for encouraging us to write it up as a book instead. We also owe a huge debt of gratitude to Roy Pea, an editor of the Learning in Doing series. Roy has encouraged this book from the beginning and provided helpful comments and critique that improved initial drafts. We would also like to recognize Sofian Ouled Amor and thank him for his graphic expertise. Thanks are also due to Simina Calin, our editor at Cambridge, and Jeanie Lee, her editorial assistant, for guidance and expertise in preparing the manuscript for production.

The most abundant thanks are due to Mrs. Glenda and her students, whose work together has inspired me over these past 15 years. It is a privilege and honor to have been present for the unit of study that we describe in this book. We hope that this iteration is taking us closer to more fully representing the power of what Mrs. Glenda accomplished with the students in her classroom. Mrs. Glenda has read versions of this manuscript and provided feedback and consultation throughout the writing process. We want to thank her for this continued conversation about teaching and learning and for providing us with such an outstanding example of teaching.

Finally, Véronique and I wish to thank her brother, Gregory, for his editorial skills and extraordinary support of this work. I would like to thank my husband Todd and children Madeline and Isaac who inspire every aspect of my life and work. Todd has been inordinately patient with my obsession with this project over many years. Maddie and Isaac have provided important diversions from the work as well as very personal motivations for me to see this project through to provide a more complete account of learning.

Leslie Rupert Herrenkohl & Véronique Mertl
Seattle, Washington
December 2009

How Students Come to Be, Know, and Do

Introduction

A true and complex understanding of another's thought becomes possible only when we discover its real, affective-volitional basis.

(Vygotsky, 1987/1934, p. 282)

... with respect to the aims of education, no separation can be made between impersonal, abstract principles of logic and the moral qualities of character. What is needed is to weave them into unity.

(Dewey, 1933, p. 34)

To say that the past 50 years has brought rapid advances in science, engineering, and technology is an understatement. Life expectancies have increased from 68 years in 1950 to 78 years in 2004. Engineering takes place on a miniscule scale, 1/100,000th the diameter of a human hair. Regular communication for business and pleasure, once the purview of the telephone and U.S. mail system, now takes place through e-mail and online video conferencing. However, in the midst of unstoppable progress in science and technology, one thing has remained the same.[1] European American women and people of color continue to choose physical science, engineering, and technology careers at much lower rates than European-American men. The question is why?

Lack of access to knowledge and skills is the most common explanation for why European-American women and people of color do not choose physical science, engineering, and technology-related careers. Some believe that increasing access to key coursework and knowledge will shift career choices among underrepresented groups. However, over the past 25 years, attempts to increase access to

[1] See Stine, D.D. & Matthews, C.M. (2009). The US Science and Technology Workforce. Congressional Research Service Report for Congress.

knowledge has not led to appreciable change in the population of people choosing career paths in science, engineering, and technology. One might argue that changes in access take time, and that we must continue to increase opportunities for underrepresented groups to gain knowledge and skills and wait for the impact on career choices. But, access to knowledge and skill is only part of the explanation.

Choosing a career engages personal inclinations and ambitions and reflects cultural and social expectations about the kinds of people who assume particular positions within American society. In light of these factors, the access to knowledge explanation is too narrow and explains too little. A new explanation is needed that is more holistic and reflective of the social, cultural, and personal nature of pursuing a career or enrolling in a course of study. In this explanation, the central focus shifts from knowledge to people in contexts over much longer periods of time, where knowledge is one part of a much larger picture. Intervening to support students of all ages to study physical science, engineering, and technology becomes a matter of introducing them to an initially unfamiliar world, providing opportunities to see how this new world connects to the personal worlds they already know, and encouraging them to become engaged participants who in turn change the intellectual, social, and cultural landscape as a result of their work.

We take the approach that engaging students of science, engineering, and technology is a matter of developing people while expanding their knowledge and skills. Our central argument is that to fully understand human learning both in and out of school, we must go beyond ways of knowing and doing to identify the ways of being a person in the world that emerge and guide human activity. Learning from this broad view is as much about the complex interaction of personal and collective interests, intentions, emotional commitments, and beliefs about how to be a person in science as it is about personal and collective ways of knowing and doing science. Our approach embraces learning as a human science.

Our book focuses on one classroom of racially, ethnically, linguistically, and socioeconomically diverse fourth graders and their science teacher to make the case for learning as a process of being, knowing, and doing. The book begins with a theoretical account of learning from this broad view. In subsequent chapters, we analyze how the classroom developed into a socially and emotionally supportive and intellectually rigorous place to learn science. We also provide case studies of four students to follow their trajectories through the classroom lessons and begin to understand how they came to see science as a part of themselves. Our intention is to build a robust, holistic model of learning that honors the complexity of being a scientific thinker and respects long-held insights from Vygotsky and Dewey that thinking is more than a cognitive act.

To Be, To Know, and To Do: An Example

To better understand what we mean by developing people as well as knowledge and skills, we provide a short example from a science unit on balance and building. Through participation in a study to test strategies to increase students' engagement in science, these diverse fourth graders and their teacher discussed complex science concepts and used experimental science and engineering approaches to investigate problems. The excerpt below took place on the eleventh day of a 12-day instructional unit on balance and building. The investigation involved building a tipi using the concepts of tension and compression to guide the design. Just before the excerpt below began, Rosie and Rich had completed a common classroom routine, reporting about their predictions and theories, their results, and the relationship between their predictions, theories, and results to the rest of class. During the report, Rich vocally shared his theory but Rosie did not fully articulate hers. As reporters, Rich and Rosie answered questions from the audience once they finished their report. Emma and Denise were members of the audience assigned to pay close attention to the predictions and theories offered by this group. Their role as audience members was to ask the reporters questions to make sure they heard and understood *all* of the group's predictions and theories. Emma and Denise wanted to hear more about Rosie's theory.

Emma:	Did anyone else in the group have a theory?
Denise:	Rosie was gonna say one and then Rich was gonna say one. Rosie, what is your theory?
Rich:	**We already said it, I said it.**

Denise:	They were both gonna say a theory.
Teacher:	Do you think they had the same theory or different theories?
Denise:	Different.
Teacher:	Excuse me, time out there's an excellent point being made here, Denise thinks that there's two theories over here...[2]
Rich:	*I already said it.*
Denise:	What were you gonna say Rosie? What were you gonna say?
Rich:	*Everybody knows what I said, right?*
Student[3]:	No.
Student:	Shhh.
Student:	Not me, not me.
Rosie:	Well, I don't know which one [previously discussed theories] because [pause]...
Denise:	Why did you think that was gonna happen?
Rich:	*Because we didn't even start yet when we predicted.*
Denise:	**You made your theory, I want to hear Rosie's.**
Rosie:	Ok, it's just that if Rich didn't cut this (the straw in the middle of the tipi), it wouldn't came out like this.

Sophisticated reasoning is evident on many levels in this short interaction. First, Emma and Denise as students were asking reporters about their ideas – something that is quite atypical in most elementary classroom contexts. This is often viewed as the teacher's role. Emma and Denise also approached their questioning in a way that revealed a deep understanding of theories and theory building. Both students probed the group for what they perceived to be different theories offered by Rich and Rosie. Emma and Denise recognized that they did not understand the alternative theories offered by this group. The teacher marked this important point and drew

---

[2] A few turns related to a mispronounced name have been deleted here.
[3] In cases where a student's voice could not be identified with certainty, "Student" will be used.

other students' attention to it. As Rosie struggled to articulate her theory, Denise again demonstrated a sophisticated understanding of theory by prompting Rosie with a question. She asked, "why did you think that was gonna happen?" This guidance helped Rosie formulate a response that would count as a theory (i.e., something that explains why or how) in their classroom context.

One could argue that this discussion of how students negotiated knowledge would be a fine place to begin and end an analysis. Embedding this excerpt within a larger analysis of how students' notions of theory building and evaluation developed across all days of instruction would provide a richer picture of students' struggle to understand and negotiate theory building as a key scientific practice. This is the approach we have taken in the past (see Herrenkohl & Guerra, 1998; Herrenkohl, Palinscar, DeWater, & Kawasaki, 1999; Kawasaki, Herrenkohl, & Yeary, 2004). However, the analysis above seems meager given the richness of the interaction. What else is going on in this excerpt?

Take the interaction between Rich and Denise, for example. Denise is an African American girl who was not afraid to take risks and make mistakes. Rich is a European American boy who often challenged other students' ideas.[4] As Denise asked Rosie to articulate her theory, Rich tried to stop her effort by asserting that he had spoken for his group. Denise was not to be deterred. She persisted in asking Rosie for her theory with Rich saying "I already said it" *four times.* As Rich continued to assert himself, so did Denise. She eventually addressed his bid to speak for his entire group by saying "you made your theory, I want to hear Rosie's." In making this statement, Denise persevered and explicitly and skillfully dealt with a sticky social situation in pursuit of a central way of knowing science – generating and understanding alternative or competing theories.

Take Rosie's perspective too. What must it have been like to be in her shoes? She is a talkative and engaged Latina who asked others many questions. Other students, however, did not always respond to her ideas in the same manner. In this case, Denise made an enormous

---

[4] Profiles of these students are presented in detail later in chapter 4. The descriptions provided here are based on these analyses.

effort to give Rosie the floor to explain her thinking. Rosie benefited from Denise's firm and direct approach with Rich, ultimately gaining an opportunity to express her ideas. All the other students witnessed this interaction and watched Denise publicly validate the need to hear Rosie's alternative theory.

What about Rich? His ongoing attempts to speak for others were tempered by Denise's skillful comment, which recognized his perspective ("you made your theory") while also insisting that he join the group in giving Rosie the floor ("now I want to hear Rosie's"). He accepted Denise's recommendation and yielded the floor to Rosie allowing her to share her theory.

And finally, let's discuss Emma. Emma is a quiet and shy European American student during whole-class time and has more absences than most students due to a medical condition. It was Day 11 of instruction and this was the first question she asked in the whole-class context. She voluntarily decided to join the larger whole-class conversation by initiating an important line of questioning in science.

It is clear even in this short example that to talk about the students' learning in terms of knowledge and skills alone diminishes and dismisses some truly profound and complex human learning experiences. Denise's persisting to understand the group's perspectives, Rich's yielding the floor, Rosie's articulating an alternative theory, and Emma's asking her first question are all crucial dimensions of these students' learning experiences in school science. Their development as people who practice school science was happening alongside and in conjunction with their new ways of knowing and doing science. Yet, our own work and the field in general provides inadequate understanding of how students emerge as participants who use their knowledge and skills in powerful ways. Our accounts of learning lack explanatory power when we focus only on knowledge and skills and neglect aspects of students' development as participants who actively negotiate the scientific process.

These omissions are the impetus for this book. Our contention is that as students become knowledgeable in new areas of study, they are also becoming certain kinds of people in relation to that subject matter, one another, teachers, parents, the larger community, and their future selves. These ways of being are often left out of our accounts of students' learning in school. Students develop and refine ways of being including interests, motivations, affective orientations toward learning, and personal and social values about what is worth learning and if, how, and why one ought to put certain knowledge and skills into practice. If we are to fully and completely understand human thought and learning, we must engage these processes of being alongside and in conjunction with knowing and doing.

Why Ways of Knowing, Doing, and Being?

We use the terms ways of knowing, doing and being to highlight the active and dynamic nature of learning. Our perspective is that knowing is an activity, a process that resides in practices that are shared by people and accomplished by using tools inherited from our cultural legacies. Ways of knowing and doing is a simple and clear way to express this general idea. Literatures related to school-based learning including subject specific learning (Rutherford & Ahlgren, 1990; Shulman & Quinlan, 1996), learning sciences and cognitive approaches to education (Bruer, 1993; Sawyer, 2006), and sociocultural approaches to learning and development both within and outside of school (Lave, 1988; Moll & Greenberg, 1990) use terms like ways of knowing, habits of mind, and funds of knowledge to connect individual knowing processes to valued cultural and social activities. We will use the terms ways of knowing and doing to capture this kind of valued social and cultural activity. In our case it will include conceptual and epistemological practices that characterize reasoning in school science. These practices are distributed across people and features of the school setting such as values, tools, and common classroom routines and practices.

Ways of being include interests, motivations, emotional commitments, and personal and social values about what is worth learning and how or why one ought to put certain knowledge and skills into practice. At the most coarse grain size, ways of being are patterns of acting and speaking that identify who a person is and what she values in a specific context at a particular point in time. Borrowing from Hicks (1996), we define ways of being as the expression of "a person in relationship within the everyday world of historical contingencies and emotional and moral commitments." (p. 108) Ways of being do not reside in individual heads and hearts. Rather, they emerge from and are negotiated in social interaction using culturally available tools, including ways of knowing and doing. Studying learning becomes a process of understanding the dynamic relationship between interests, motivations, emotional commitments, values, and ways of knowing and doing to more fully explain students' actions in world.

We have elected not to use the terms identity or identities, although some authors we will draw upon to discuss our work use these terms. There are several reasons we made this choice. First, identity has become a widely used term with multiple meanings depending on author and audience (see Hicks, 1996). Second, theoretical schools that have used "identity" often give priority to either the individual or the social world but not often to the dynamic interaction that exists between them. This is not true of the work on identity that most influences our own (see Greeno, 2002; Holland et al., 1998; Holland & Lachicotte, 2007; Lave & Wenger, 1991). However, in the literature there is a tendency to treat identities as fundamentally properties of individuals (Erikson, 1950, 1968; Harter, 1999; Marcia, 1980) or social worlds (Gergen, 1991; Goffman, 1959) rather than an interaction between individual and social world. Third, and most importantly for us, identity is a noun and therefore gives the impression that it is a product or thing and not a process. Our choice of "being" allows us to emphasize a dynamic process instead of what might be misconstrued as a static product (identity or identities).

Situating Our Perspective in Broader Discussions of the Purpose of Education

We began the book with a discussion of how current approaches to workforce development in physical science, engineering, and technology continue to focus on knowledge and skills as leverage points for changing the demographics of people choosing these careers. We argued that the access to knowledge approach is inadequate even when workforce development is considered the goal of education. When the purpose of education is defined as creating an educated citizenry prepared to participate in a democracy, a purpose that Dewey and many contemporary philosophers espouse, our broad view of developing people who put knowledge and skills to use is paramount. We see our perspective as situated within these larger movements in the social sciences and humanities to create education for democracy that reflects Aristotelian notions of human flourishing.

Several perspectives in this movement have been important to the conceptualization of our broad view of learning. Toulmin (1992), drawing from Aristotle, argues that today's philosophers and scientists need "intellectual grasp of a theory (episteme), mastery of arts and techniques (techne), and the wisdom needed to put techniques to work in concrete cases dealing with actual problems (phronesis)" (p. 190). The first two dimensions, knowledge and skills, are familiar to those who study learning from social science points of view. What might be less familiar is an emphasis on phronesis, or the idea that practical wisdom guides the use of knowledge and skills as they are applied to actual problems. Phronesis transforms knowledge and skills from decontextualized tools to concrete opportunities for action. People use tools to accomplish personal, social, and cultural goals that are embedded within webs of values and beliefs. Actors are located in particular social and cultural contexts, bring personal motives, feelings, beliefs, and agendas, and use specialized ways of knowing and doing to accomplish their tasks (Burke, 1945).

In applying this approach to education, Nussbaum's (1997) perspective is similar to Toulmin's. She suggests higher education must "cultivate humanity" by supporting students to develop knowledge and skills together with practical wisdom to put knowledge and skills to good use. She argues, "becoming an educated citizen means learning a lot of facts and mastering techniques of reasoning. But it means something more. It means learning how to be a human being capable of love and imagination" (p. 14). Her concern is that knowledge and skills are becoming increasingly separated from contexts of application and action within curricula in higher education. Creating people and communities that can "genuinely reason together about a problem, not simply trade claims and counterclaims" should be a central goal of higher education (p. 19). She concludes her book by saying, "It would be catastrophic to become a nation of technically competent people who have lost the ability to think critically, examine themselves, and to respect the humanity and diversity of others" (p. 300). She argues that higher education must address this issue of practical wisdom as well as knowledge and skills to meet the needs of twenty-first-century college students. While looking forward, Nussbaum is also pointing back to Dewey's vision of weaving abstract principles of logic together with moral qualities of character.

Flyvbjerg (2001) builds on the philosophical turn to phronesis through his attention to power as it affects putting ways of knowing and doing into action within the social sciences. Flyvbjerg argues that we must consider how power is omnipresent and negotiated, a perspective inspired by Foucault and his question, "how is power exercised?" (Flyvbjerg, 2001, p. 118). This work is important because conflict and resistance and other affective elements that often remain hidden can become more easily revealed when power is examined (John-Steiner, 2000; Herrenkohl & Wertsch, 1999). Some work has taken up this stance within classrooms, examining how power is negotiated among students, teacher, and content during classroom lessons (Barron, 2003; Cornelius & Herrenkohl, 2004; Engle, de Royston, & Langer-Osuna, 2008; Matusov, 1996; K. O'Connor, 2003). We take this approach here as well, recognizing that as ways of being, knowing, and doing are enacted, they will come into conflict and require ongoing negotiation. These relationships of power are not stable. They can shift and change since there are, in Foucault's (1999) words, "many points of resistance." (p. 477).

If we re-examine our classroom example from this phronetic stance, Denise and Emma addressed an actual problem (not understanding what they think are two theories offered by Rosie's and Rich's group) using practical wisdom that reflected a powerful scientific way of knowing (Emma initiates and then Denise persists with a line of questioning about alternative theories). This all happened in an ongoing social negotiation that was fluid and changing, that required moment-to-moment decisions and adjustments. Rich was trying to dissuade Denise from pursuing her line of questioning and assert himself as sole spokesperson for his group, so this process involved conflict and power. This was delicate but enormously fruitful work with fourth grade students demonstrating scientific ways of knowing, doing, and being central for an educated citizenry.

Our approach provides an account of learning that engages with this larger discussion about what it means to emerge as people through the process of learning in our contemporary world. We consider ways of being as a centerpiece for phronetic analyses of school science learning. To accomplish this task, next we outline the sociocultural perspective upon which our ideas are built. Although a focus on ways of being is supported theoretically within this tradition, we argue that it is not well incorporated into accounts of school-based learning at the analytic level. Our approach will demonstrate one way to go about conducting analyses of being together with the more common foci of knowledge and skills.

Sociocultural Approaches to Learning and Development

Vygotsky (1978, 1987/1934) and scholars following in his footsteps argue that learning is fundamentally a social, cultural, and historical process (Cole, 1996; Wertsch, 1988). In schools, this means that students learn particular ways of knowing and doing that are valued by some stakeholders in our society. Explicit and tacit social and academic norms guide classroom and school level interactions and expectations. Broader institutional, political, and cultural contexts shape district, school, and classroom policies and practices as education is continually debated and defined in the public and legislative spheres. In essence, from this sociocultural view, schools are complex and contested places where different constituents' values, goals, and purposes come into contact. Students learn inside of a system that itself is constantly undergoing change.

To explain students' learning at the classroom level, sociocultural theory emphasizes the social dimension of learning and the tools used for thinking and communication. These tools, such as language, mathematical and scientific notation, structures of argument, and other shared representational forms are a cultural accomplishment and inheritance (Cole, 1996; Tomasello, 1999). Contemporary ways of knowing and doing are therefore guided and supported by these important culturally developed and historically vetted tools. In Wertsch's (1998) terms, human thinking can be characterized as "mediated action" or the "irreducible tension" (p. 25) between a person and the cultural ways of knowing and doing she employs. Therefore, even school children are engaged in cultural processes when they are learning in their classrooms. Students use a constellation of valued ways of knowing and doing as they learn in their classrooms and schools.

Vygotsky's theory emphasized human learning as a complex whole, recognizing the individual, social, and cultural together (Van der Veer, 2007; Veresov, 1999). Vygotsky also sought to bring together intellectual and affective processes stating, "There exists a dynamic and meaningful system that constitutes a *unity of affective and intellectual processes*" (Vygotsky, 1987/1934, p. 50, italics in original). Bakhurst (2007) argues that Vygotsky "insisted on the importance of emotions in guiding and informing cognition . . . Emotion may be essential to our responsiveness to reasons, in part because it facilitates the intellect, and in part because some reasons can be discerned only by beings with the appropriate emotional sensitivity" (p. 68). For Vygotsky, considering affective and intellectual processes together was a necessary part of explaining human learning and development.

This approach is further evident in Vygotsky's analysis of the basic flaws in psychological paradigms that were most prominent during the time he lived and worked. From Vygotsky's point of view, isolating the intellectual from what he called "the affective and volitional" created limited views of thinking. He expressed serious reservations about this approach.

> The inevitable consequence of the isolation of these [affective and volitional] functions has been the transformation of thinking into an autonomous stream. Thinking itself became the thinker of thoughts. Thinking was divorced from the full vitality of life, from the motives, interests, and inclinations of the thinking individual. Thinking was transformed either into a useless epiphenomenon, a process that can change nothing in the individual's life and behavior, or into an independent and autonomous primeval force that influences the life of consciousness and the life of the personality through its intervention. (Vygotsky, 1987/1934, p. 50)

It is within this dichotomy of "thinking is nothing" and "thinking is everything" that Vygotsky entered with his own approach to embody thinking in people who have particular motives, interests, and inclinations and who are situated within particular historical, cultural, social, and affective contexts. He resisted the prevailing trends and argued for a more holistic approach to human learning (see also Daniels, Cole, & Wertsch, 2007; Van der Veer & Valsiner, 1991). He appreciated and situated the messy intersection of intellect and affect within larger social and cultural contexts without arguing that any one dimension determines the others. This was a radical idea when Vygotsky first proposed it, and it continues to be a radical idea today. According to Van der Veer (2001), Vygotsky's concept of *perezhivanie*, or "the way the environment is reflected and refracted in the [person's] mind" (p. 101) provides one way to understand the functioning of this complex whole.

Contemporary Perspectives on Vygotsky's Holistic Theme

Contemporary theorists borrow and build on Vygotsky's notion that traditional dichotomies of individual/social and intellectual/affective must be considered together. Lave and Wenger (1991) emphasize that learning is a process of becoming a more fully recognized participant in a particular social world. This involves shifts not only in knowledge and skill but also in social membership, personal responsibility, and power.

Locating cognition within social practices that connect culture, local social context, and individual participants breaks down the barriers between traditional psychological categories of individual and social/cultural world. Lave (1988) writes, "Cognition in action is by nature fused with feeling since it cannot be separated from the expression and creation of value. There are a number of reasons, it seems, to give up categorizing knowledge, thinking and feeling in the image of a person and world stringently divided" (p. 182).

Holland, Lachicotte, Skinner, and Cain (1998) also contribute to building a broad view of learning through their emphasis on improvisation. Improvisation is the mechanism that creates both personal and cultural change. Holland and colleagues (1998) argue, "in our neo-Vygotskian developmental approach, thoughts and feelings, will and motivation are *formed* as the individual develops. The individual comes, in the recurrent contexts of social interaction, to personalize cultural resources... as a means to organize and modify thoughts and emotions. These personalized cultural devices enable and become part of the person's "higher mental functions," to use Vygotsky's term." (p. 100, emphasis in original). At the same time that individuals are making cultural resources personal, they are also leaving their personal "signatures" on cultural resources, contributing to the ongoing re-creation of their cultural contexts and tools. This process connects sites of personal and cultural change to continuities (or discontinuities) in time, linking past, present, and future.

Building on interpretations of Spiro (1982) and Dreyfus (1984), Holland and her colleagues also contribute to a broad view of learning through examining how expertise and interest develops together. Holland and colleagues' study of young women's approaches to romance demonstrated that "salience, identification, and savoir faire appeared to develop together in an interrelated process – a process that was continually supported and shaped in the context of social interaction" (p. 116). In other words, as women developed greater competence in navigating the romantic scene, their evaluation of the importance of romantic pursuits, their emotional investment in this activity, and their desire to continue intensified. Holland and her colleagues suggest that this kind of emotional commitment and interest is necessary to further develop expertise. Developing ways of knowing and doing is deeply and inextricably intertwined with ways of being. They mutually influence and inform one another. Holland demonstrates that ways of being are extremely important to understand if one wants to understand people's mastery of ways of knowing and doing.

This dynamic perspective on learning opens up the very idea of what it means to learn as well as the central object of learning. To learn means much more than collecting knowledge and skills, it involves whole people fully engaged in creating a life for themselves in the many places where they learn. Wenger (1998) defines learning as a process of becoming as well as knowing saying, "It [learning] is not just an accumulation of skills and information, but a process of becoming – to become a certain person or, conversely, to avoid becoming a certain person. . . . It is in the formation of an identity that learning can become a source of meaningfulness and of personal and social energy" (p. 215).

Contemporary Sociocultural Perspectives on Learning in Schools

Although it is common to find work in formal school contexts that focuses on sociocultural approaches to knowing (see Moll, 1990, 2001) there are far fewer examples of work that embraces the broader view of learning advocated by Vygotsky and contemporary scholars such as Lave, Wenger, and Holland and her colleagues. Although teacher's intuitive hunches tell them that students' ways of being are important and research-based evidence suggests that social-emotional development is linked to academic learning (Greenberg et al., 2003; Oatley & Nundy, 1996; Payton et al., 2008), there are fewer studies that try to deeply understand this connection in schools from a sociocultural point of view. In addition, although there is strong recognition that schools are cultural systems, where ways of knowing are embedded in shared social practices that can and do differ across cultures and contexts (Lewis, Perry, & Murata, 2006; Moll, 1990; Stigler & Hiebert, 1998), this approach is not often used to explicitly examine and understand students' cultural ways of being. Forging connections that examine how ways of being, knowing, and doing together account for learning in school is relatively rare.

Yet, there is a need for scholarship of this kind. Sociocultural scholars working within formal educational settings use the notion of a "community of learners" which has the potential to embrace a broader view of learning (Brown, 1997; Brown & Campione, 1990, 1994; Greeno, 1997, 1998; Matusov, 1999; Rogoff, 1994). A community of learners is a classroom structure offered as an alternative to the dichotomous adult-directed or child-centered paradigms in the literature. In the words of Rogoff (1994), "children and adults together are active in structuring shared endeavors, with adults responsible for guiding the overall process and children learning to participate in the management of their own learning and involvement" (p. 213). Brown (1997) defines a community of learners as learning environments where students exercise agency in their learning, where they reflect on their work to better understand it, where there is true collaboration, and where a shared culture emerges among the community's participants.

In communities of learners, Rogoff (1994) defines learning as a "transformation of participation" (p. 209) emphasizing the need to examine how students' roles and understanding shift over time. Analyses that examine learning as transforming student participation in school contexts are becoming more common since sociocultural approaches have gained greater recognition over the past two decades (for example see Barron, 2003; Engle & Conant, 2002; Greeno, 1998; Herrenkohl & Guerra, 1998; Moll & Greenberg, 1990; Polman, 2004; Rosebery & Warren, 2008; Rosebery, Warren, & Conant, 1989, 1992). These studies focus on the ways students' and teachers' roles shift with respect to valued ways of knowing in the classroom. They have been instrumental to investigating learning as a shared cognitive process centered on valued cultural and discursive practices. However, they leave ways of being implicit and do not address how personal and collective interests, intentions, emotional commitments, and beliefs contribute to patterns of transformed participation.

One reason for this may rest in what Packer and Goicoechea (2000) describe as the "hidden ontology" (p. 229) of sociocultural theories of learning. Packer and Goicoechea argue that sociocultural approaches eschew mind/body dualism and embrace a holistic stance on ways of being in the world (or ontology), but the assumptions behind this stance are implied rather than explicitly stated. They argue, "whereas much psychological research treats identity simply as self-concept, as knowledge of self, that is, as epistemological, the sociocultural conception of identity addresses the fluid character of human being and the way identity is closely linked to participation and learning in a community. However, the details are not always clear" (Packer & Goicoechea, 2000, p. 229). Packer and Goicoechea argue that ways of being must be treated in a more explicit manner to conduct empirical research that fully embraces the potential to understand learning from a sociocultural point of view.

This lack of clarity about ontological assumptions has had an effect on the aspects of interactions that are highlighted (or not) in analyses of classroom-based learning. Often times, intellectual and social aspects are examined in detail without attending to the ways of being that exemplify our phronetic view. Students' and teachers' personal interests and motivations, the range of emotions enacted and experienced in the classroom, values about what is worth knowing and why, actions that put ways of knowing to powerful use in the classroom, etc. are left unexamined. This is especially true in the focal subject matter content for this book — science. Long ago, Dewey (1933) argued against this view.

> .... ideas involving emotional response and imaginative projections are ulti-
> mately as necessary in history, mathematics, scientific fields, in all so-called
> "information" and "intellectual" subjects, as they are in literature and the
> fine arts. Human beings are not normally divided into two parts, the one
> emotional, the other coldly intellectual – the one matter of fact, the other
> imaginative. The split does, indeed, often get established, but that is always
> because of false methods of education. Natively and normally the personal-
> ity works as a whole. There is no integration of character and mind unless
> there is fusion of the intellectual and the emotional, of meaning and value,
> of fact and imaginative running beyond fact into the realm of desired pos-
> sibilities. (p. 278)

Dewey suggests the need to examine the ways that emotion, imagination, values, and meaning come together in scientific learning in schools (see also Alsop, 2005 for contemporary arguments for the importance of considering emotion in the learning of science). Fifteen years ago, Brown and Campione (1996) argued that the field needed a new theory of learning to help account for the richness of learning experiences they encountered and observed in their efforts to create "communities of learners" in elementary classrooms. Integrating ways of being, knowing, and doing will address this contemporary need for a new broad view of learning while drawing inspiration from foundational scholars in our field.

Our Approach to Knowing, Doing, and Being in the Classroom: Some Beginning Assumptions for a Broad View of Learning

Greeno (2002) argues that to accomplish this task of building a more robust theory of learning we must not separate students' ways of being from the content that they learn. He writes,

> We cannot relegate our understanding of students' identities as learners to the context of their learning, factoring it away from the processes and outcomes of learning per se. Instead, identities need to be considered as an integral aspect of what is learned and developed, as well as how and why learning occurs successfully or unsuccessfully as it does. (p. 17)

We adopt Greeno's perspective as a starting point. First, we believe it is necessary to investigate ways of being, knowing, and doing as intertwined strands that together weave a complex narrative of learning in the classroom (see also Gresalfi, 2009). At times it may be necessary to foreground ways of being and doing or ways of knowing and doing but our assumption is that they are always at play together. Our approach works to make sense of how students' developing competence as scientific thinkers is inextricably linked to their emotional investment in the social and discursive practices of being a student of science. Holland and colleagues (1998) suggest that this kind of emotional commitment and interest is necessary to develop expertise, that these aspects mutually influence and inform one another. Holland demonstrates that ways of being and doing are extremely important to understand if one wants to understand people's mastery of ways of knowing and doing. You cannot have one without the other. We are interested in pursuing this line of reasoning with respect to student learning in science. Analyses like this will be better suited to making ontological assumptions and processes clear, as suggested by Packer and Goicoechea (2000). They will also address Dewey's (1933) and Brown and Campione's (1996) concern that learning theories reflect the richness of classroom life so that principles of learning and strategies for fostering complex learning within classrooms can be clearly articulated and shared.

We also embrace Greeno's developmental point of view. Learning is a process not just an outcome. Much of the work in science has measured learning from the standpoint of ways of knowing that can be captured at the end of a unit of study – the conceptual and epistemological outcomes. Studies that examine processes often do so by capturing snapshots of classroom moments rather than examining sustained learning over an entire unit. We seek to better understand learning as a process over time through focusing on ways of knowing, doing, and being as they emerge in the context of learning, instead of examining outcomes alone.

By identifying these strands of knowing, doing, and being we respond to a tension raised by Nasir and Hand (Nasir, 2006; Nasir & Hand, 2006) who argue that it is often difficult to distinguish what counts as an act of learning in contrast to act of identity within school contexts. Their proposal is to methodologically identify strands related to learning and identity so their interrelationships might be discussed. In our case, we choose to call these ways of being, knowing, and doing and to locate these strands under the larger tent of what we call learning. We believe that analyses that focus on ways of being and not just ways of knowing and doing must be incorporated in any approach to learning as we have argued that education creates people as well as knowledge and skills.

Research Questions and Methodological Approach

To conduct our analyses, we drew on multiple data sources including video recordings and transcripts of classroom lessons, field notes that functioned as daily summaries, student work such as pre- and post-assessments that focused on the science content and epistemologies, laboratory notebooks that recorded small group investigations, report posters that provided a written account to use when discussing work with the entire class, and other class generated documents that helped guide the learning and thinking. Interviews with the teacher and four students were also conducted throughout the study. These interviews were audiotaped and key excerpts were transcribed.

Our analytic approach is organized around four lenses, each of which corresponds to a set of research questions and a methodological approach to investigate them. We seek to understand contextual, community, interpersonal, and personal perspectives on knowing and being in the classroom. Each analytic lens will be described in detail below. This approach is inspired by Rogoff's (1995) three planes of analysis (community, interpersonal, and personal) and the extension of her work made by the Stanford-University of Washington Collaboration Study Group (Mercier et al., 2008). This work on collaboration employs the four analytic lenses we use in this study: context, community, interpersonal, and personal.

Rogoff's approach was a starting point for our research because she recognizes the dynamic relationship between the individual and the social world and conceptualizes learning as a developmental task involving a "transformation of participation" (1994, p. 209). Rogoff argues that development must be considered across all analytic planes simultaneously. Thus, the planes she identified are not viewed as separate analyses but rather as parts of a whole with particular aspects "spotlighted" for the sake of analytic convenience. This approach is absolutely essential to her work and to ours. We use Rogoff's framework as a basis to integrate our attention to ways of being as well as ways of knowing and doing. We will pay particular attention to ways of knowing and doing as well as ways of being or patterns of participation that explicitly engage affect, motivation, interests, conflicts, and values about putting ways of knowing and doing into practice.

The Context Lens: Locating Being, Knowing, and Doing within a Web of Values, Principles, Practices, and Tools

Rogoff calls her first plane of analysis "community" and identifies apprenticeship as the central developmental process on this plane. Our approach, following the work of the Stanford-University of Washington Collaboration Study Group (Mercier et al., 2008) separates this analytical lens into two parts. We name the first part context and the second part community. O'Connor's (2001) perspective on proscriptive versus critical approaches to situated learning encouraged us to disentangle context and community levels of analysis. Context refers to the more standard proscriptive or idealized version of a physical and social setting and the values, principles, and practices it should espouse. Community reflects the critical view that what is essential to understand from the context is how a community emerges from the context in ways that might be different from the abstract ideal. The community lens will be discussed below as we closely associate this lens with the interpersonal one. The contextual lens describes the physical space (the architectural elements of a setting, number of participants, etc.), the cultural-historical environment (e.g., the institution, time constraints, technical tools) and the initial norms and practices designed for the context (e.g., rules, values, participation structures). This lens may reflect a certain amount of idealism if separated from the other analytic lenses as it could be thought about as a "wished for" existence – a way in which people in power in a context want people to be, to know, and to behave within that context. Analyses at this level represent a more institutional and sociological perspective on the resources available within the cultural and social context apart from thinking about how these resources are actually taken up and used within a classroom community. Key analytical questions for the contextual lens are: *What are the major physical, social, and demographic characteristics of the institutional context and where is it situated? What are the most important values, principles, practices, and tools for knowing and doing in this context? What range of emotions is expected within the classroom context? What values or distinctions of worth exist to guide conduct within the institutional context?*

The context lens examines in the abstract what it means to be, to know, and to do within a context. In a school and classroom, some aspects of the context may be considered generic (i.e., not dependent on subject matter) including ways of being a student and a class to maintain a climate of respect, roles, and responsibilities of teacher and students (Hickey & Schafer, 2006), methods to deal with problems or concerns, strategies to ensure equal access and fairness for all (Cohen, 1994). Other aspects are subject matter specific. For example, key terms and concepts, "cognitive values" (Goodnow, 1990; Lampert, 1990) about what counts as legitimate problems and elegant approaches to solving them in a particular domain, and modes of engagement that are productive and unproductive in furthering knowledge in an area of study (Forman & Ansell, 2005).

Mechanisms or tools and practices for communicating shared values and routines are essential to understand as a part of the larger context. Direct and indirect means of communicating these values can be identified including oral or written text-based or graphic messages available to classroom members, physical arrangements of classroom space, and types of activities and ideas that are engaged within the classroom.

The Community and Interpersonal Lenses: Locating Being, Knowing, and Doing as They Emerge through Interpersonal Negotiation of Values, Principles, Practices, and Tools

Whereas the contextual lens focuses on the kinds of values, principles, practices, and tools that are explicitly being espoused or designed by people in power to foster newcomers' apprenticeship, the community and interpersonal lenses seek to understand what emerges when these contextual resources are actually put into place inside a particular classroom community. These analyses will form the core of our work. As members of the classroom community take up (or argue against, push back on, etc.) particular values, principles, practices, and tools, they inevitably bring to life what would otherwise be viewed as abstractions. To fully understand apprenticeship, we must understand the resources available in the context as well as the processes by which new members come to understand and participate together and become a community. Central values, principles, practices, and tools are interpersonally negotiated among participants and this has specific consequences on what emerges within the community. These moment-to-moment interpersonal interactions actively create community (O'Connor, 2001). Therefore, we choose to focus on these lenses together. Through examining interpersonal interactions and negotiations it becomes possible to see how the community is built from them over time, including the kinds of emergent values, principles, practices, and tools that come to define the community and the ways that it may differ from the idealized contextual view. Key questions for the community lens include: *What central values, principles, practices, and tools for knowing and being emerge within the community over time? What range of emotions emerges within the community over time?*

Are emotions discussed and if so, how? How are values and distinctions of worth negotiated and enacted to create expectations for community thinking and behaving?

The interpersonal lens focuses on the moment-to-moment interactions that unfold in the classroom. Discourse analysis is the primary method to examine interpersonal interaction (Gee, 1990; Hegedus & Penuel, 2008; K. O'Connor, 2003; Wortham, 2004, 2006; Yamakawa, Forman, & Ansell, 2008). "Negotiated participation" is the focal developmental process for this lens. Patterns of interaction are at the center of analyses, spotlighting the place where individuals' purposes, inclinations, intentions, emotional commitments, and ideas come into contact with each other and with the values, principles, practices, and tools described in the contextual lens. Here ways of being, knowing, and doing are actively constructed and deconstructed, enacted and contested, adopted or rejected. We will use turns as our unit of analysis for this plane. Turns involve speech as well as nonverbal forms of communication including eye gaze, body movement, and positioning. Questions that anchor analyses on the interpersonal plane include: *What types of interpersonal interactions and social arrangements unfold in the classroom context? How do moment-to-moment interactions shape and structure students' interests, motivations, and affective orientations toward learning? How do classroom interactions manifest personal and social values about what is worth learning? What do classroom interactions reveal about how and why community members put certain knowledge and skills into practice? Do community members resist or argue against central values, norms, and practices about ways of knowing, being, and doing? If so, how?*

As a starting point for our analyses on this plane, we draw on the work of Edwards and Mercer (1987) and Nasir (2006) who argue that the meaning created and shared by community members must be investigated and understood. In Edwards and Mercer's (1987) terms, there is a kind of "common knowledge," or in our terms "common ways of knowing and being," that are shared and negotiated within a community. And, as Nasir (2006) points out, although it is tempting to make assumptions about certain kinds of practices and values and what they mean from *outside* of a community, by doing this one risks misinterpreting what is happening *within* that community. Therefore, the meanings that matter are the ones that are generated, examined, negotiated, and contested by the participants themselves (see also Esmonde & Langer-Osuna, 2007). Students and teachers play crucial roles in this process of negotiating meaning, as is also highlighted in the work of Dyson (1995), Forman and Ansell (2005), Gutiérrez and Stone (2000), Lee (1995, 2001), Rose (1995), Rosebery and Warren (2008), Rosebery, Warren, and Conant (1992).

The Personal Lens: Locating Being and Knowing within a Person's Experiences across Time

As people participate in events, they communicate, negotiate, and coordinate with others and then take up things that influence how they will participate in future situations. Following individuals' patterns of participation and engagement over time provides a powerful account of individual learning and development. Rogoff (1995) argues that "focusing on how people participate in sociocultural activity and how they change their participation demystifies the processes of learning and development" (p. 159). The focus of analysis on this lens is change in individual participation over time, identifying ways of knowing and being that are nested within interpersonal, community, contextual lenses discussed earlier. Key questions that anchor analyses on the personal lens include: *What ways of being and knowing do individual students espouse and what patterns of interaction do students enact at the beginning of the classroom experience? How do individual students' initial ways of knowing, interests, motivations, and affective orientations toward learning change across the duration of the classroom experience? How do the students talk about and reflect on their own participation in the classroom?*

This plane of analysis provides an account of being, knowing, and doing at the level of a particular individual. Our case studies (Merriam, 1998) analyze how a particular student interacts with others over time to improvise his or her own experience and contribute to the creation of the cultural resources within the classroom community (Holland et al., 1998). Identifying how ways of being, knowing, and doing are initially manifest for a particular student and how she or he improvises over time reveals a learning trajectory for that particular student.

A Broad View of Learning

In an article that examines her use of a cultural modeling approach to teaching literature classes to underachieving African American high school students, Lee (2001) argues that the human dimension of teaching cannot be forgotten. Each day the students in her class resisted her attempts to teach them. As the teacher, she had to "appreciate the humanity of these young people, their innate talents, their infinite ability to learn, grow, and develop." (p. 133). She also had to demonstrate that there was no amount of resistance that could change her belief that they already thought in powerful ways and that they could continue to learn to think in new and compelling ways. She asserts that, "this was one of the most powerful tools in the teacher's pedagogical toolkit" (p. 133).

We embrace Lee's stance that to teach means to support students as people as the first step to understanding them as thinkers and actors in the world. This book examines what it is like to be a student with emotional commitments, interests, values, beliefs, and ideas at this particular cultural and historic moment in time. It also explores what it is like to be a dedicated teacher who cares that students develop into productive, responsible, caring human beings as well as good thinkers. It embodies the belief that the public school classroom represents, however imperfect it may be, a microcosm of democracy and an effective place for all children to develop into productive, competent, and fulfilled thinkers, people, and citizens. This human side of learning can easily be lost in our attempts to segregate what might be considered "soft" outcomes of learning from the real business of schooling – academic achievement. This book contributes to discussions that reframe learning as a human science and restore ways of being as a centerpiece of our educational philosophies and practices. In a small way, we will begin to take up how students become people in the world as well as thinkers in subject matters between the hours of 8:50 A.M. and 3 P.M., 180 days a year, for (if they stay in school) 13 years of their lives. Students' and teachers' ways of being, including their personal interests, cultural backgrounds, and motivations, must be considered together with academic content and concepts, classroom values, expectations, and patterns of interaction to present a holistic picture of student learning and development. Together these aspects form the dynamic cauldron of the classroom where students and teachers create their classroom culture, their knowledge, and themselves.

1   The Context Lens

The analyses that we discuss in this book are part of a study that was designed to encourage students to think scientifically using explicitly defined social roles and intellectual practices. This chapter provides important background information about the context of the data collection, including demographic information on the school and the study participants. Information about the genesis of the study, its purpose, and its central guiding principles are provided. Classroom-based materials and practices are described.[1] Key analytical questions for the contextual plane are: *What are the major physical, social, and demographic characteristics of the institutional context and where is it situated? What are the most important values, principles, practices, and tools for knowing and doing in this context? What range of emotions is expected within the classroom context? What values or distinctions of worth exist to guide conduct within the institutional context?*

The School

Data collection took place in a public science and technology magnet school situated in the poorest quadrant of a New England city. Approximately 800 children attended the school, making it (at the time of data collection) the largest public elementary school in New England. As a neighborhood magnet school, it welcomed children who lived in the neighborhood and attracted students from throughout the city as part of a voluntary de-isolation plan. A rich racial,

---

[1] See Herrenkohl, L. R., & Guerra, M. R. (1998). Participation structure, scientific discourse, and student engagement in fourth grade, *Cognition and Instruction*, 16(4), 431–473 for more detailed information about the context, method, and materials used during the initial data collection.

ethnic, and socioeconomic mix of students resulted. In 35 classrooms from preschool through grade 6, about half of the student population was children of color. About one-quarter attended a Spanish bilingual program that was housed within the school. Approximately 90 percent of the students qualified for free or reduced lunch. This school was one of five in this community that had established a Professional Development School with a neighboring university. At the time of the study the school had been in operation almost 2 years.

Students received regular classroom instruction in science (beginning at grade 2) using the Complex Instruction model (Cohen, 1990). Complex Instruction was developed based on sociological principles that emphasize the importance of multiple abilities beyond the usual reading and computation, distribution of tasks among students, cooperation to complete tasks together, and equal access to materials and ideas for all students regardless of their social status in the classroom. Lesson formats involved whole-class, teacher-led introductions followed by small-group work time and whole-class reporting sessions. The participants in our study engaged in Complex Instruction lessons before our research began. Our study involved students in extra lessons outside of their regular classroom time with a teacher who was not their regular classroom teacher.

The Teacher

The teacher, Mrs. Glenda, was the science facilitator at the school. She assisted the classroom teachers with their work on Complex Instruction. She had been in this role for almost 2 years at the time of the study. In her former position, she taught in a self-contained special education classroom and was a master special education teacher with 18 years of experience. She had regularly used science as a vehicle to engage and inspire her special education students and was recognized at her school for this work. When asked why she dedicated a significant amount of time to teaching science to special education students, she was very clear. She said that many of her students came to her believing that they were, in their words, "dumb" in literacy and math. Mrs. Glenda noticed that her students did not have well-formed evaluations of their capability to understand science.

For Mrs. Glenda, science became the preferred vehicle to support students to develop strong knowledge and skills across the curriculum and build confidence that would help undo their negative self-assessments in literacy and math. Mrs. Glenda's students enjoyed and adored her. Sometimes her students resisted a transition to a regular education classroom by acting out, purposely not doing their best, or outright refusing to participate saying that they wanted to return to Mrs. Glenda's classroom.

Mrs. Glenda did not have any specialized training in the sciences. She had worked with professional scientists in the past, bringing them into her classroom to work with her students, but she had not formally studied science herself. However, science fascinated Mrs. Glenda. She found that it was as engaging for her as it was for her students. She described herself as a learner beside her own students.

Mrs. Glenda and the first author (Leslie Rupert Herrenkohl) had known one another for about 2 years at the time of the study through involvement in the university–school partnership. Mrs. Glenda readily agreed to participate as the teacher in this research study when Leslie proposed the idea to her. Mrs. Glenda and Leslie worked together to conduct the study and to think about how what they were doing could help students and teachers at the school. Although Mrs. Glenda had worked as science facilitator for almost 2 years at the time of the study, the school was large and the population of students shifted so she did not know all the students who participated in the study before it began. She recognized and had regular contact with some of the students as a result of her past role as a lunch detention supervisor, as the teacher of older siblings or relatives, and as the current science facilitator who assisted students' regular classroom teachers. However, she was teaching the participating students in a classroom setting for the first time.

The Students

Student participants were drawn from two classes of fourth graders at the school. Transition bilingual students were included in the pool of potential participants whereas students residing solely within the bilingual program were not included. Participants were selected using two criteria. First, two fourth grade teachers nominated students in their classes whom they perceived as "average" students. Then, students who were nominated by their teacher and represented the statistical average within their classes on the basic battery score of the Metropolitan Achievement Test 7, Fall, 1993, were chosen to participate. This procedure was followed to allow us to create two comparable groups of students. Eleven students from one fourth-grade class and 13 students from the second class participated. Students were assigned to participate in one of two different classroom groups using a matched pairs procedure, again attempting to ensure that the groups were similar with regard to gender and racial composition as well as standardized test scores. As a result, the students did not necessarily know one another or have experience working together before our study began.

The analyses presented in this book focus on one group of students. This group of students was introduced to cognitive tools for thinking like a scientist and intellectual roles to support students to ask reporters questions about their work (see the next section for discussion of this approach). The other group of students was introduced only to the cognitive tools. We discuss just one of the groups here because we found that the intellectual roles had a significant impact on student participation and engagement (see Herrenkohl & Guerra, 1998 for analyses of both student groups). Students who participated in the study using intellectual roles asked 226 questions during reporting whereas students in the group without specific intellectual roles asked only four questions during reporting. Due to this significant difference, we focus on what happened in the group of students who used the intellectual roles (see Table 1 for information on students).

The Researcher

Under the auspices of the school–university partnership, Leslie worked as an ethnographer at the school where the study took place. She had been working there for almost 2 years at the time the research study took place. Her role at the school up to that point was to document the schoolwide implementation of Complex Instruction. In

Table 1. *Student demographics: Ethnicity, language status, and original fourth grade class*

Student code names	Ethnicity	Language status	Original fourth grade class
Rosie	Latina	Bilingual	1
Tammy	European American	Monolingual	2
Olivia	African American	Bilingual	1
Denise	African American	Monolingual	1
Emma	European American	Monolingual	1
Steven	European American	Monolingual	1
Raul	Latino	Bilingual	2
Carson	European American	Monolingual	1
Dai	Asian American	Bilingual	2
Rich	European American	Monolingual	2
Qing	Asian American	Bilingual	2
Christie	European American	Monolingual	2

this role, Leslie made several observations that supported the instructional approach in the research study discussed here. She noticed that students were struggling to make intellectual connections and arguments across activities in the same unit. Students were not always building a coherent sense of an intellectual domain. Rather, students found it challenging to relate activities to one another in meaningful ways. In addition, teachers reported that as time went on during science units, reporting sessions became shorter and shorter rather than longer and more complex. Reporting sessions did not become more elaborate as the teachers had expected. Students were having a hard time sustaining interest and focus and were not asking questions of other groups or making connections to their own investigations. These observations provided the foundation for the development of an initial set of values and principles that would guide the design-experiment study discussed here.

Guiding Principles for Learning

Because the design experiment to be conducted was Leslie's dissertation, she played a significant role in defining at the outset the central values and principles that would be presented to students. She had some practices in mind to test. She would see if these practices were effective in supporting students to engage more fully in the social and intellectual work in classroom science lessons. Leslie identified key values and principles that might help address concerns that the teachers had raised and she had observed in her time in classrooms. The key principles included in the design experiment study were: (1) provide cognitive support to help students understand what to focus on across investigations within the same unit, (2) interrupt typical patterns of classroom interaction where teachers ask questions and students answer them and establish new patterns where students take up the role of questioning, (3) assist all students in generating, discussing, and refining ideas together, (4) create different kinds of classroom arrangements and tools to further support the multiple abilities approach within Complex Instruction and assist in documenting student thinking over the course of a unit.

Once the basic principles were established, a set of practices was developed to embody these values and principles in the classroom. There were three key practices created to support this work: (1) cognitive tools to support students to understand what to focus on across investigations in the same unit, (2) procedural, small group, and intellectual roles to interrupt typical patterns of classroom participation and provide more support for all students to take up the roles of questioner, commentator, and constructive critic in the classroom, and (3) classroom configurations, including both small-group and whole-class work time and "public text" as a way to engage ideas and document joint work over time.

For the group of students we discuss in this book, the cognitive tools and intellectual roles were combined in an approach we call intellectual role-taking, depicted in Figure 1. The foundation of intellectual role-taking is identifying central ways of thinking within a discipline, or what we conceptualized as cognitive tools. Three focal practices of thinking like a scientist were introduced to students: (1) predicting and theorizing, (2) summarizing results, and (3) relating predictions and theories to results. This was an idealized version of a particular kind of experimental scientific thinking. As such, it served as an early introduction and guide for students. These

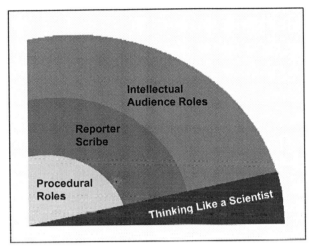

Figure 1. Intellectual Role-taking Model.

practices were targeted because children as well as adults struggle to coordinate theories and evidence, a crucial element of complex scientific thinking. Building on the work of Palincsar and Brown (1984), a primary objective of this approach was to exteriorize metacognitive processes and embed them in roles. In Figure 1, these practices are represented by the triangular wedge that serves as the foundation for three kinds of role-taking.

The first kind of role-taking, procedural roles, occurred in small-group work settings. A common feature of many cooperative learning programs, these roles were designed to distribute procedural tasks such as getting materials, cleaning up, keeping time, and facilitating the group's activity. The roles shifted daily so that each student had an opportunity to carry out different tasks. These roles were important for young students as they minimized disputes and disagreements and made transitions to important intellectual activities possible. During small-group work time, the students used the procedural roles and the practices of thinking like a scientist to guide their progress through an investigation.

The next set of roles, the reporter and scribe roles, functioned to connect the small-group work to the whole-class reporting sessions. Often used as a procedural role, reporting was quite a difficult task for students to take on individually. Therefore, in this model, two students in each small group acted as reporters and two students acted as scribes who prepared the materials that the reporters used to explain their group's work to the entire class. During the report preparation time, the scribes and reporters talked together to create representations that reporters subsequently used during the whole-class reporting session. To structure their report, the students focused on the practices of thinking like a scientist, which served to provide necessary information to the audience. These roles rotated to provide students an opportunity to function as both reporters and scribes for their small group.

Intellectual audience roles, the whole-class component of this model, involved assigning students in the audience the responsibility for checking reporters' presentations of predictions and theories, summaries of results, and relationships between predictions, theories, and results. These roles structured discussion of important epistemological ideas for young science learners. Students needed support to understand what kinds of thinking practices were important to privilege in science (Cobb & Yackel, 1996). These roles gave specific guidance to students who began to learn techniques for how to have discussions about their small-group investigations. Additional support was provided through the use of a "questions chart" that publicly documented and displayed students' brainstormed questions for each of the intellectual audience roles. Students were prompted to think about the kinds of questions they could ask if their job was to check predictions and theories. This chart was posted in a prominent place during reporting time and often served as a scaffold for students as they began taking on intellectual audience roles.[2] All three sets of roles rotated regularly so that every student could experience each one.

We also used the practice of publicly documenting theories (what we called our "theory chart") over time to support students to reflect on the range of theories offered and to compare and contrast their own and others' previously suggested theories. The students used this chart as a central reference for their classroom discussion. These

---

[2] The genesis of the chart itself will be discussed in the analyses. Originally it was intended for brainstorming, but it became a chart we displayed on a daily basis. The students initiated this activity and it has since become a regular feature of this approach.

practices were designed to support metacognitive reflection on conceptual and epistemological ideas of the unit.

The Curricular Materials and Activities

The materials for this study were modified from the school's standard science curriculum, Finding Out/Descubrimiento (FO/D, DeAvila, 1987). FO/D was originally developed as a hands-on discovery curriculum designed to enhance students' exploration, questioning, and cooperation. At the school, other resources often supplemented this curriculum to provide more focused instruction in scientific concepts. We followed the same approach, making modifications to a unit on balance and building to focus students' attention on important concepts in science such as the multiplicative rule of torque, tension, and compression. This approach allowed for the construction of a unit that reflected developmental research on the conceptual understanding of balance scales (Butterfield & Nelson, 1991; Siegler, 1985). The series of lessons addressed problems using balance scales, pan balances, and a seesaw, and then applied newly acquired concepts around weight, distance, and balance to building and investigating models (building two soda straw bridges and a tipi) during the final sessions. The modified curriculum supported students to develop theories and models to support their reasoning (Lehrer & Schauble, 2005).

The Daily Schedule

The research study took place in addition to the regular Complex Instruction science lessons. Students participated in extra science sessions with Mrs. Glenda to test the use of the new practices discussed in the previous section. The study consisted of 12 sessions each approximately 60 minutes in length. The first activity session elicited baseline explanations from the students without any instruction about ways of thinking like a scientist or the intellectual roles. Eleven activity sessions followed that introduced content together with scientific ways of thinking and intellectual roles. On Day 1, the teacher introduced the ways of thinking like a scientist and

Balance and Building Investigations across Baseline to Day 4

Samples of balance scale[3] and pan balance[3] activities to experiment with weight and distance from the fulcrum.

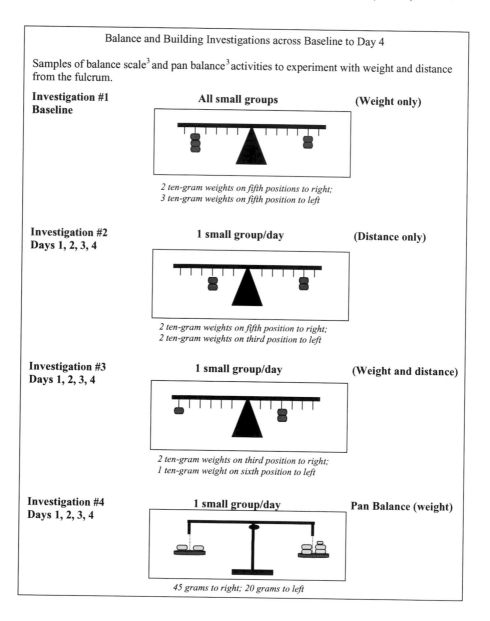

Investigation #1
Baseline

All small groups

(Weight only)

2 ten-gram weights on fifth positions to right;
3 ten-gram weights on fifth position to left

Investigation #2
Days 1, 2, 3, 4

1 small group/day

(Distance only)

2 ten-gram weights on fifth position to right;
2 ten-gram weights on third position to left

Investigation #3
Days 1, 2, 3, 4

1 small group/day

(Weight and distance)

2 ten-gram weights on third position to right;
1 ten-gram weight on sixth position to left

Investigation #4
Days 1, 2, 3, 4

1 small group/day

Pan Balance (weight)

45 grams to right; 20 grams to left

[3] On the cards, the representations of the balance scale and pan balance always had a fulcrum fixed in the center with the arms straight across (not leaning left or right) to allow the students to predict possible outcomes.

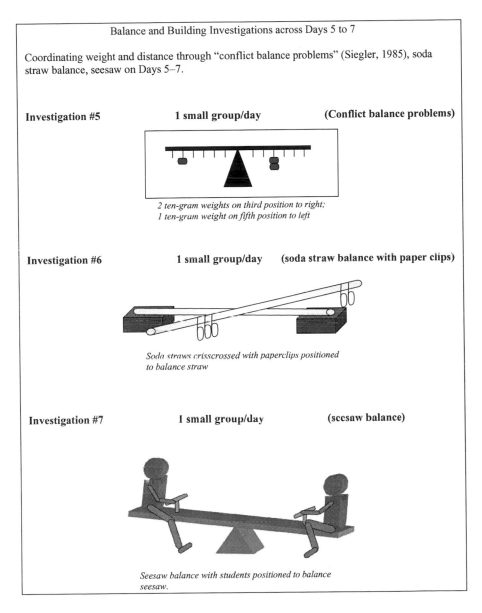

Balance and Building Investigations across Days 5 to 7

Coordinating weight and distance through "conflict balance problems" (Siegler, 1985), soda straw balance, seesaw on Days 5–7.

Investigation #5   **1 small group/day**   **(Conflict balance problems)**

*2 ten-gram weights on third position to right;
1 ten-gram weight on fifth position to left*

Investigation #6   **1 small group/day**   **(soda straw balance with paper clips)**

*Soda straws crisscrossed with paperclips positioned
to balance straw*

Investigation #7   **1 small group/day**   **(seesaw balance)**

*Seesaw balance with students positioned to balance
seesaw.*

Balance and Building Investigations across Study Days 8 to 11

Applying new concepts of balance to building models – soda straw bridges and tipi on Days 8–11.

Investigation #8 **1 small group/day** **(Bridge of strength)**

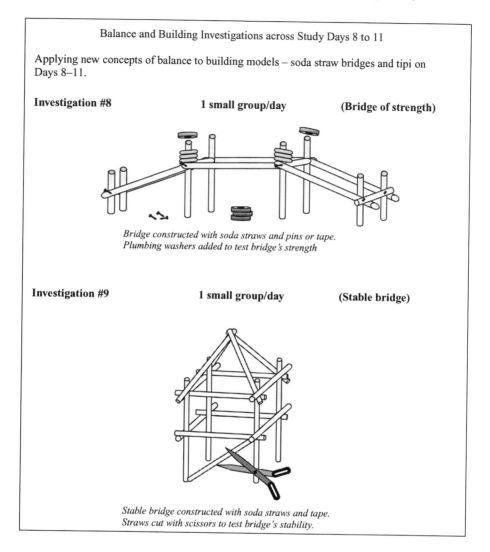

Bridge constructed with soda straws and pins or tape.
Plumbing washers added to test bridge's strength

Investigation #9 **1 small group/day** **(Stable bridge)**

Stable bridge constructed with soda straws and tape.
Straws cut with scissors to test bridge's stability.

Balance and Building Investigations across Study Days 8 to 11 (continued)

Applying new concepts of balance to building models – soda straw bridges and tipi on Days 8–11.

Investigation #10   **1 small group/day**   **(Tipi)**

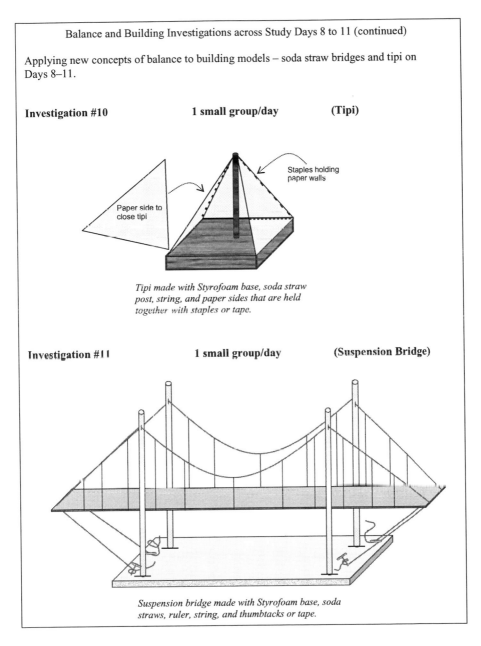

Staples holding
paper walls

Paper side to
close tipi

Tipi made with Styrofoam base, soda straw post, string, and paper sides that are held together with staples or tape.

Investigation #11   **1 small group/day**   **(Suspension Bridge)**

Suspension bridge made with Styrofoam base, soda straws, ruler, string, and thumbtacks or tape.

intellectual roles for the first time, spending approximately 20–25 minutes on this, and allowed the students to ask questions, comment, and discuss the ways of thinking with the whole group. Once the large group discussion was completed, the students began their first round of experiments on balance in their small groups. The students finished the first round of investigations on Day 2 and prepared and presented their first oral reports to the class. For the first round of investigations, students took 2 days to do what would thereafter be done in 1 day. Given the novelty of these techniques and procedures, it was necessary to give the students extra time to become accustomed to the new tools, practices, and roles.

On Days 3 through 11 the daily schedule included a teacher introduction, student small-group work time, and reporting. The 15-minute teacher introductions occurred until Day 7.[4] The teacher presented and then reviewed the concepts of thinking like a scientist and/or intellectual roles. The teacher used a number of techniques to involve students in these discussions including sampling student work, whole-group construction of examples, as well as comments, questions, and recapitulations of explanations from previous days.

On most days, after the introductory teacher remarks and whole-class activity, students were given 25 minutes to complete their activities in their groups and compose written explanations. Students worked every day to complete a different activity in the same small groups composed of four students. Leslie and Mrs. Glenda formed the small groups randomly much as any teacher would do when faced with a new class. During the small-group activities, the teacher was available for answering questions and providing guidance. In addition, students had reminder sheets that outlined the ways of thinking like a scientist, posted signs, and laboratory notebooks to help them record critical information for their explanations. Students' official laboratory notebooks contained all their written work, such as process notes taken during the activities, diagrams, drawings, explanations, and revisions. While students were preparing their oral reports, they had access to large chart paper that they

---

[4] The students asked the teacher to reduce the amount of time she spent orienting them at the beginning of the lesson so they could spend more time reporting and discussing at the end of class. The genesis of this suggestion will be presented in Chapter 2.

could use to write, draw, demonstrate, and explain their perspectives. During this time, the two scribes in each group were asked to record important information, diagrams, and other information on the chart paper. The two reporters were responsible for delivering the oral report. Mrs. Glenda reviewed student procedural role assignments before small-group activities.

After the students completed activities and explanations, the last 20 minutes or more of each session was devoted to students' oral reports to the class. Before reports began, students were handed an index card with their assigned intellectual audience role. Each small group was to present each day. However, on Days 2 through 6, all three groups of students did not offer reports due to time constraints. The new ways of thinking like a scientist and adopting intellectual audience roles required more time and practice during these first few days. All other days (baseline and Days 7 through 11) all three reports were presented. The challenges students faced while beginning to use these new ways of thinking will become evident in the Chapter 2 through an analysis of the community.

Ways of Being as Background

Ways of being are conspicuously absent from our discussion of the context. We do not want to rewrite history now to make it seem as if we had thought about these issues in advance of commencing the study. Our initial focus was on how ways of knowing and doing would be negotiated socially in the science classroom. We took an approach that centered on the social construction of knowledge and practices rather than the social construction of people. Most educational work focused on changing students' conceptual and epistemological practices shares this same basic omission – leaving the ways of being as unexamined background rather than indispensable foreground. For our purposes, discussion and analyses of ways of being will be conducted in the chapters that follow this one – Chapters 2, 3, and 4. Discussing ways of being in these chapters allows us to accurately represent the moments where we first paid attention to them. We recognized as the study proceeded that there was a need to think more carefully about exactly what we were asking students to do, how this impacted business-as-usual in the classroom, and what students were learning as a result.

In spite of our lack of explicit reflection on ways of being in advance of the study, it is important to surface implicit, unspoken ways of being within the context of school that the students confronted as we asked them to take up new roles in the classroom. Our designed values and practices focused on ways of knowing and doing but also positioned students to become different kinds of students, students who ask questions of each other and make connections across different activities in science. These new expectations contrasted with typical cultural models of American schooling.

By the time students are in fourth grade, they are intimately familiar with traditional classroom recitation patterns where the teacher asks a question, the student responds, and the teacher evaluates the student's answer (Mehan, 1979), placement and achievement tests, and other indicators that suggest that the purpose of school is to "get the right answer." Despite all of the effort in the United States since the cognitive revolution to move schooling toward a focus on process as well as product, there is a strong and enduring "right answer" model that is housed not necessarily in individual classrooms but in the bricks and mortar of the institution itself (Becker, 1982; Dreeban, 1968). "Getting right answers" and "being right" are standards by which students judge each other and themselves (see also Cohen, 1984, 1994). This model was implicit in our study classroom as well. "Right answer" assumptions were especially evident in the classrooms when the pretest for the study was administered. Some students expressed frustration and concern that they were not able to produce the correct answers to the problems that were posed. The teacher had to reassure them that it was not a test (we did not call it a pretest with the students) and that it did not matter if the responses they produced were correct. Unfortunately, the students may have received mixed messages from this common research practice. Our purpose was not to have students produce "right answers"; in fact we were explicitly preparing to challenge that notion in our classroom-based instruction.

Our work in the classroom challenged this "right answer" model of schooling. It focused on the development of students' theories over time as they discussed their ideas in both small-group and whole-class settings. A large part of this work was in revising and discarding theories that did not seem to account for data. There were no "right answers"; there were only theories that were better or worse at explaining the evidence that students gathered through their investigations. Too often school science is conceptualized as a passive process of receiving facts from textbooks and teachers or simply observing and recording information accurately (Songer & Linn, 1991). Yet, professional science is an active and flexible set of conceptions that can and do change over time (Carey & Smith, 1993). Science is a body of representations about the world that is developed and constantly scrutinized within scientific communities (Driver et al., 1994). This was the model we introduced to the students, one that was more commensurate with the work of actual scientists but did not conform to a standard "right answer" approach that many students had come to expect in school.

In addition to our emphasis on revising theories as a central feature of scientific thinking, our model also involved several other key assumptions about theories and theory building including: (1) theories tell WHY something happened. This distinguishes them from predictions that identify WHAT one thinks will happen, and (2) theories need to have an evidence base gathered through empirical testing. Theories and evidence must be coordinated. Kuhn's (1992) work has demonstrated that both children and adults have a difficult time developing sound arguments supporting their claims with evidence, even in domains that are familiar to them. Furthermore, Schauble and colleagues (Schauble, 1990; Schauble, Klopfer, & Raghavan, 1991) suggest that upper elementary students struggle to systematically generate and interpret evidence. The students in these studies engaged in a kind of confirmation bias and therefore often made invalid judgments about disconfirming evidence and supported interpretations with the use of invalid evidence. This raises an important issue for teachers and researchers who view science as a form of argument where data are used to bolster theoretical positions (Driver et al., 1994; Kuhn, 1993). Learning science as a process of revising theories over time is not an easy or straightforward process, but rather one that requires extensive support and explicit instruction in the classroom. Our approach made several key assumptions about theories and set out to create classroom supports to assist students to develop more robust theoretically based arguments about balance and building. However, as would be predicted based on previous studies, this new approach proved challenging for the students.

Given this discrepancy between the standard "right answer" approach and our alternative "developing theories" model and the research findings that suggest that students have difficulty creating and modifying theories using evidence, the dilemmas our students faced as they took on their roles within the new study classroom seem predictable in hindsight. Creating shared understanding and definition of terms and concepts like prediction, theory, results, and what it means to relate predictions and theories to results proved difficult. There was also discomfort and loss of face associated with student reporters taking questions from other students, especially when reporters did not have a ready "right answer." These dilemmas produced many opportunities for conflict and tension, for a renegotiation of cognition and emotion inside new distinctions of worth, and for subject matter to come into contact with students' conceptions of themselves and their abilities.

2 How Ways of Knowing, Doing, and Being Emerged in the Classroom

Interpersonal Interactions and the Creation of Community, Part I

Educational research has demonstrated that educational designs can be quite different from their enactment. Therefore, designed principles and practices must be considered in emergent terms. Even though the designed features for this study were linked to observations made by teachers and researchers in the school, until they were placed into actual classrooms they existed only as models that may remedy some classroom dilemmas. Using a design-experiment approach (Brown, 1992), Leslie and Mrs. Glenda decided to see what would happen if new tools and strategies were introduced in the classroom. Leslie put significant thought into classroom participation structures and tools that could help students better understand the science and take more responsibility for questioning one another about the their ideas in science. Leslie and Mrs. Glenda did not plan for possible challenges the students would face as they navigated new ways of being that were associated with these new ways of knowing. What happened when Mrs. Glenda set the designed values, principles, and practices described in Chapter 1 with the students as key members of the community? How did new ways of being come together with new ways of knowing in the context of the classroom?

In this chapter and Chapter 3, we focus on interpersonal interactions as they unfolded and created a classroom community where students questioned each other about their scientific ideas. In this chapter we focus on how students took up their new roles as "questioners." In Chapter 3, we discuss how this new way of questioning spawned several other significant areas of development with respect to ways of being, knowing, and doing in the classroom. To conduct these analyses, we primarily draw on classroom transcripts and interviews with the Mrs. Glenda. We will also present some quantitative data about students talking and questioning patterns. We examine the interpersonal and community lenses together because the community emerges from the moment-to-moment interpersonal interactions over time. First, we will describe what happened day-to-day as the Mrs. Glenda introduced the new approach to science in this classroom. Questions that anchor these analyses using the interpersonal lens focus on negotiated participation as the central developmental process: *What types of interpersonal interactions and social arrangements unfold in the classroom context? How do moment-to-moment interactions shape and structure students' interests, motivations, and affective orientations toward learning? How do classroom interactions manifest personal and social values about what is worth learning? What do classroom interactions reveal about how and why community members put certain knowledge and skills into practice? Do community members resist or argue against central values, norms, and practices about ways of knowing, being, and doing? If so, how?*

After these analyses of daily interactions are presented, a summative section will address the community lens that focuses on key questions including: *What central values, principles, practices, and tools for knowing and being emerge within the community over time? What range of emotions emerges within the community over time? Are emotions discussed and if so, how? How are distinctions of worth negotiated and enacted to create expectations for community thinking and behaving?*

The Teacher's Role

Mrs. Glenda's role requires special consideration before we begin the process of analyzing what happened in the classroom. During the first few days of the study, it quickly became apparent that new ways of being were totally intertwined with the new ways of knowing and doing we were attempting to foster in the classroom. The students brought these issues to the fore with their explicit questions, puzzled looks, and uncomfortable silences. Although ways of being were not explicitly discussed in the planning phase of the project, Mrs. Glenda brought a tacit wisdom of practice into play as she worked together with the students. For her, considering ways of being was part of the practice of teaching itself. She also brought some specific personal theories about student learning and development to her reflections about what was happening in the classroom. Some aspects of these personal theories and her wisdom-of-practice are evident in her explicit comments made during interview sessions. Her personal beliefs and practices are also visible in the moment-to-moment interaction with the students in the classroom. Mrs. Glenda responded on the spot to the issues students raised about how to conduct themselves when new values and beliefs about students' roles as science questioners were in place. The students, together with Mrs. Glenda, were instrumental in creating opportunities for new ways of being to be addressed and values and practices around them to be negotiated and established. Mrs. Glenda's framing and perspective were explicitly felt during the early days of the study but continued long after the students had taken up their roles as questioners of one another.

Mrs. Glenda had strong beliefs about equity and equal access to airtime in the classroom for all students. Mrs. Glenda's general philosophy about equity came from her extensive experience with special education students. However, she had also received training in Complex Instruction (Cohen, 1990) and believed that status was conferred in many ways in the classroom and that it had an impact on students' access to materials and ideas in the classroom. She worked hard to be sure that she was aware of these dynamics and intervened when necessary to address student status and access to learning opportunities. Mrs. Glenda used the metaphor of a funnel to talk about how she viewed her role with students. Some students enter the classroom at the "wide end of the funnel" sensing that all the classroom airtime was theirs for the taking. She talked about her role to help channel their exuberance enough to make room for others. Mrs. Glenda reported that other students enter the classroom at the narrow end of the funnel and need their horizons broadened so that they can find their voice to make contributions to class discussion. She saw the teacher's role as making assessments of these needs and being sure to fulfill them. Some students needed to move from the wide end of the funnel to the middle and others needed to move from the narrow end to the middle so that they could all contribute and learn together.

Mrs. Glenda also believed that it was essential to use what she called "kid language" or "kid text" in the classroom. She reported introducing new terminology to the students when "I've either seen them do it or I've heard them do it or I've heard them talk it through without using the word. And at that point I'm comfortable giving them the word without making it into a vocabulary lesson." In addition to offering the students helpful terms to describe their ideas, she also listened closely to their terms and ideas and frequently repeated them to build students' understanding in their own words.

Changing students' ways of being in the classroom was an area that Mrs. Glenda believed to be enormously challenging. As a special education teacher, she had seen many students struggle with traditional school tasks in reading, writing, and math. She used science as a vehicle for learning across the curriculum in her special education classroom as a result. During a reflective interview after the baseline day, Mrs. Glenda noticed and commented on issues that went well beyond the ways of knowing approach we were taking and moved fluidly into a ways of being perspective. She was discussing some students' frustration with the pretest. These students had difficulty getting their ideas down in writing and were worried about being wrong. Mrs. Glenda had to reassure one student in particular that "no this isn't a test, no it doesn't matter whether or not this is right." She suggested a modification that might help him in future situations, "as a special ed teacher my guess is that if he's having a hard time getting it down on paper, why can't he just talk it through?" This is what students would be doing with one another during classroom lessons so Leslie explored this suggestion with Mrs. Glenda. Leslie asked Mrs. Glenda what she thought would happen for students like this when they were asking questions of other students using their intellectual audience roles during reporting time.

Leslie: Can you give me a sense of what a kid like that would do in the role of having to talk it through, of having to ask questions of other people? How would a kid interact with a responsibility like that? Would it be too much for him or [inaudible]?

Mrs. Glenda: [he might] benefit and [inaudible] but it might be very hard for him to do because I [3 second pause] **I mean I don't think he sees himself as somebody who could do that so you are really going to be changing who he is in a bigger way and that would be hard.** On the other hand, once he has it and he's sorta fluent in it then I think you've given him the best thing you could give him because now publicly he'll be able to ask the right questions and maybe when it's his turn to explain he'll be able to do it so that his peers see him in a different light. And, he still may fudge when he gets to [writing on] paper, but that's ok.

Mrs. Glenda broadens the conversation well beyond ways of knowing. She explicitly commented that much of what was going to be possible depended on how this student saw himself as a person. And, changing that meant something much bigger than changing his way of thinking. But, if it succeeded, then it would give him tools to participate in a new and confident way with peers in the classroom. From these comments, it is very clear that Mrs. Glenda was already operating from a ways of being stance on learning. Her experience as a special education teacher helped her tune in quickly to students' emotional experiences, especially around their self-evaluations. She was easily able to assess what students needed, both academically, socially, and emotionally in this context. She wanted them to know that she believed in their ability to succeed.

Mrs. Glenda used several different pedagogical techniques to support the students throughout their learning: (1) modeling by providing explicit examples of thinking, doing, and being to students, (2) questioning students to better understand their thinking, their level of comfort with particular roles, their understanding of other students' ideas, etc., (3) offering students props to help them explain their thinking, (4) redirecting students' ways of knowing and being to support successful social and intellectual interaction when tensions developed, (5) positioning members of the classroom, including

herself both to support and to stretch confidence and current capabilities, (6) prompting students to repeat what other students said
in their own words, (7) revoicing or repeating students' ideas in the
context of a discussion to emphasize that student thinking in students' words mattered and was the center of the work in the classroom (O'Connor & Michaels, 1993), (8) naming particular ways of
being and knowing – both directly in talk and indirectly through her
actions, and (9) acknowledging individual and group contributions
to the class process of trying new roles and developing new ideas.
Many of these pedagogical techniques are discussed in Tharp and
Gallimore (1988). The analyses presented here are not focused on
the teaching techniques that are used, nor will they present all the key
sections that would be necessary to understand Mrs. Glenda's pedagogy. However, this background knowledge is essential to understand the interpersonal and community lenses as Mrs. Glenda played
a crucial role in setting expectations for classroom norms, values, and
emotional climate through her beliefs and practices.

Students Questioning Other Students about Their Scientific Ideas: Shifting Ways of Knowing, Doing, and Being

As Figure 2 indicates, students asked 226 questions over the course
of the study. The amount of questioning initiated by each student
varied. What the graph cannot present, however, are the initial challenges that all students had to overcome to become questioners.

The following analysis traces the development of the capacity to
question, as a way of being, knowing, and doing in this classroom
context.

Prelude to Audience Members Questioning Reporters: Reporters questioning the audience.

Baseline Day: "But we want them to guess."

On the baseline day (the first day the students and Mrs. Glenda
met together), Olivia and Denise presented their second balance
scale problem to the class, 1 ten-gram weight on the third position
to the right and 2 ten-gram weights on the third position to the

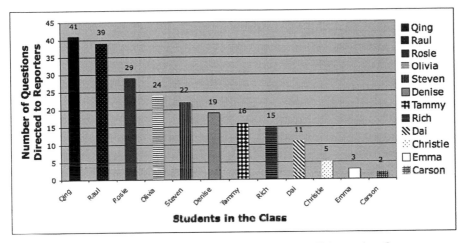

Figure 2. Graph of Number of Questions Students Directed to Reporters. The graph shows the number of questions each student in the class asked the presenting groups over the course of the 12 sessions.

left.[1] The students had not yet received any guidance about how to organize reports or how to proceed with the actual reporting to the whole class.[2] The girls decided they wanted the students in the audience to participate in demonstrations as they reported about what they had found during group time. So they began by setting up their balance scale problems and asking audience members to predict the outcome.

Denise	Which side will go down?
Mrs. Glenda:	Oh so you guys didn't get to it?
Olivia:	No, yeah, we did.
Denise:	**But we want them to guess** [Qing raises her hand]
Mrs. Glenda:	Qing
Qing:	I think the two will go down.
Olivia:	Two ten-grams on the number three

[1] See the curriculum outline, Chapter 1 p. 36 for a graphic representation of the balance scale and some sample problems that students completed for each investigation.

[2] The baseline was designed to see what students would do without instructional support. Although Mrs. Glenda was there and provided the activities and general support, she did not make any suggestions about what students were to focus on or how they should report out to each other.

Denise:	Two here
Olivia:	On number three on the left
Denise:	Put one here
Olivia:	No, this is left [touches the scale] and this is right [touches], one ten-gram weight on number three on the right.
Denise:	And put one right here, which side do you think will go down?
Raul:	Wait, how many are over here anyway?
Denise:	Which one do you think will be heavier?
Comment:	Kids are facing in toward the group and trying to respond to their questions.
Denise:	How many people think this side will be heavier?

In presenting their report, Denise and Olivia asked the class "which side will go down?" This was an unusual move because students typically *told* the class about their activity and what they found out during their regular science classes. It surprised the Mrs. Glenda, who first thought that maybe they did not have enough time to complete all the problems included in their investigation. Olivia reinforced that they did complete the work. Denise clarified their intentions, stating "but we want them to guess." Right away hands went up in the audience and the students physically turned their bodies toward Denise, Olivia, and the balance scale. Many students became part of the interaction as Denise and Olivia set up the problem. Denise was determined to get responses from her peers, so as the interaction continued, she asked her question three more times and even insisted, with the help of Olivia, that everyone listen. After Denise and Olivia finished reporting, the remaining group picked up on their approach to reporting and also set up their problems and asked the audience to guess the outcome. Mrs. Glenda closed the lessons by saying:

Mrs. Glenda:	...the third thing that I wanted to say that I thought was very interesting today is um since this really wasn't defined as FO/D [curriculum] and um there wasn't any real, gee this is how you do

this reporting business. It's interesting how some of you decided that you would just give a straight report and how some of you decided that it would be a better report if you used a visual and if you got your friends involved in guessing, so I thought that was pretty interesting.

In a debriefing meeting immediately following this session, Mrs. Glenda commented about the students' thinking and their ways of organizing themselves during this session that involved no explicit teacher direction. First she said that it had been difficult not to intercede to provide guidance to the students. Then, she quickly turned to how the students organized their reporting session.

Mrs. Glenda: They just modeled what happens in [their regular] classrooms and my introduction [earlier that day] when they did [reporting out]. Asking each other, "What do you think?" [laughs]

Mrs. Glenda was struck by how the students' enacted instructional models they had seen in the past, commenting on this directly to them as well as in the reflection discussion with the researcher. Denise and Olivia used Mrs. Glenda's instruction that day as their model for how to report. They asked the other students questions and got them involved, just as Mrs. Glenda had done in her introduction to the day's lessons. Another group followed their lead and used the same approach. This was an early sign that at least some of the students in this class were going to be interested in asking each other questions and taking on roles that were normally enacted by the teacher. Other students used what happened in their regular classrooms as a model to support reporting out. They prepared a report and then read it aloud to the other students.

In the reflection discussion with Leslie, Mrs. Glenda commented on the students' intellectual focus on predictions.

Mrs. Glenda: And they are really kinda stuck on prediction.
Leslie: What do you mean by stuck on prediction?
Mrs. Glenda: Well maybe, this morning when I was walking around [giving the pretest in their classrooms],

well this definitely happened in classroom 2 so it will be interesting to see which kids were doing it. In the classroom 2 group I read your directions [for the pretest] exactly and then I had like four or five hands go up for clarification and then I went around individually and then oddly enough one was Qing, one was Rich, one was Curt [boy from the other group in the study] and then I think there were two little boys that I don't know who they are. And there was a lot of concern about predict, I mean is that a guess? What's going to happen if I'm right or wrong? That sort of thing so they might have been stuck on that even though the main thrust of this [the baseline session] was explanation. I think at this point explanation means, "what did you predict?" Period. I'm not sure if that is what they gave you back in writing [on the pretest] but...

Leslie: I'm guessing...

Mrs. Glenda: Probably they did.

Leslie: Yeah, so that's interesting. So from [what you experienced] today you're saying that the kids' definition of explaining consists solely of predicting?

Mrs. Glenda: Yeah, yeah.

Leslie: Oh that's interesting.

Mrs. Glenda: Yeah and whether or not that is right or wrong cuz as they would see their predictions either come true or be falsified [in the demonstration that was included in the pretest]...if they got it right they were like "yes!" well, "what's the next one" while the kids who didn't get it right were laying on their desks or something like that.

Mrs. Glenda was beginning her informal assessment of students starting points with respect to ways of knowing in science. From her observations during the administration of the pretest and during this first baseline day, she believed that the students generally conceptualized scientific explanations as predictions that had been tested. If students made correct predictions they were excited because they had correct explanations. If they did not have correct predictions they were dejected because their explanations were obviously wrong. These beginnings were important to Mrs. Glenda and to the study that was aimed at testing an approach to support students to engage ways of knowing in experimental science, with explanation as the crux of the work. What is understood in this exchange between Mrs. Glenda and Leslie is that the students were not yet showing signs of providing reasons why predictions might be expected (a form of explanation), a central feature of sophisticated scientific thinking.

Immediately following these comments about predicting, Mrs. Glenda also described her first impression of the students and their ways of being.

> *Mrs. Glenda:* This is a real solid representation of what every teacher faces. I mean, this is not a group of really good bright kids who are going to do the teacher's bidding. These are a group of kids who are going to make you earn your spurs all the way through. And so there will be some testing behaviors which probably will at times um (pause) outshine the amount of (pause) whether it's theorizing or um or sort of "ah ha" moments (laughs).
>
> *Leslie:* So you think this is gonna be somewhat of a challenge, this particular mix of kids?
>
> *Mrs. Glenda:* Yeah, I mean, I don't think it's an impossibility [to work with them] at all, I just think it's for real. I mean this is what teaching [at this school] is like. Actually, I think this is what teaching anywhere is like.

Mrs. Glenda's comments are important and interesting for at least three reasons. First, this group of students was a good representation from her point-of-view of what teaching at this school was like. These were not hand-selected model students who would make the task of teaching easier. Second, she knew that this fact was perhaps a disadvantage because of the shorter time span for the study when compared to beginning with a new class at the start of an academic year. Her comments contain both possibility and concern about whether or not the intellectual tools and social roles could be put to an adequate test in the time allotted if the students were engaged in testing behavior. Third, Mrs. Glenda was clearly focused on ways of being and their potential interaction with ways of knowing right from this first meeting with the students. In making her first assessments, she was taking into account how the students' testing behaviors might impact their intellectual work of theorizing (something she had already noted was lacking in their scientific explanations) and achieving some insight in their thinking or what she called "ah ha" moments. Although Mrs. Glenda and Leslie did not discuss ways of being as part of the design phase of the work, it was an inevitable and inescapable part of the classroom experience and Mrs. Glenda's reflections, even before the new social and intellectual roles were introduced in the classroom.

Introducing the Ways of Thinking Like a Scientist and the Intellectual Roles

Apprenticing the students to the new values, principles, and practices began after the baseline day, during Mrs. Glenda's daily orientation to the class or right before they began their reporting time. These times involved teacher direction and definition, introducing new terms and practices to the students. This was followed by ample support as students took on these new practices during reporting out. We will begin the process of examining these interactions here as we trace how the principles and practices we designed were enacted early on in the classroom.

Day 2: "This is the first time, yes this is hard, the hardest job is not the reporter's job, the hardest job is all of our jobs here." Mrs. Glenda introduced the cognitive tools to the students before the beginning of their first set of investigations. The cognitive tools included: (1) predicting and theorizing, (2) summarizing results, and

(3) relating results back to the original predictions and theories. Then students worked together in small groups to complete their activity and compile a report to be presented to the class. This first set of activities took two days to complete. Before the beginning of Day 2, Mrs. Glenda reviewed the three cognitive tools (what she called the three steps) with the students.

Mrs. Glenda: Let's go through the three steps. Remember in your journals, you should have the first step, you should have your predictions and you should have your theories you wanna make sure that they're there this morning. The prediction was the guess or the "I think" part. I think this will happen. And the theory was the why you thought it was gonna happen. This was before you did your activity, right? Also, after you've done your activity, you should have in your notebooks, you should have a summary of your findings and results. This is really what happened. And, it's up to you how clear you need this to be for everyone to understand. If you wanna say, first I did this, second I did this, then this happened and remember we came up with don't put the "who cares" stuff in there. Remember what who cares stuff is?

Students: Yes.

Student: Stuff that really [inaudible].

Mrs. Glenda: Yes, ok. And we had here [pointing to the chart where she has written this information with their assistance] the main stuff and the order. And then the last step, you wanna make sure that after you've got your prediction down and your theory and your results that you go all the way back and you have your third step you wanna relate your predictions and theories to your real findings. Did what you have for results, does that support your theory? Or does that make your theory not there anymore? So, I looked through some of these [science journals] and I know we didn't have time to finish so I would like to really seriously when you get your journals back to look through and see, "Do I have the first step? Do I have the second step? Do I have the third step? If you are stuck that's why I'm here. I'm very happy to come around and help you get your steps in order. Then we'll do your reports. Ok? Ok.

The student did not ask questions, but took their notebooks and began working in their small groups to go over their three steps so that they could prepare their reports.

When small-group time was complete, the students gathered in a central place to begin reports. Mrs. Glenda explicitly reminded the students about both the cognitive and the social responsibilities that they would assume during the reporting session they were just getting ready to begin. For the first time, they would be using the cognitive tools together with the intellectual audience roles. While reporting groups shared their reports, each student in the "audience" was given a card with a particular intellectual audience role based on the cognitive tools. The audience members were asked to make sure the reporters were (1) predicting and theorizing, (2) summarizing results, and (3) relating results back to the original predictions and theories.

Mrs. Glenda:	There are going to be reporters coming up here and giving their explanations, however, unlike FO/D [curriculum] the rest of you guys do not go on snooze control, ok?
Tammy:	What is that?
Mrs. Glenda:	This does not mean that the reporter comes up and the rest of you guys wait your turn, ok you all have a job and your [index] card tells you your job, so if you have a card that says predicting and theorizing, when the reporter is up here, you listen to see is there a prediction in their explanation and is there

a theory, and I put some things up here that might help us for today, is the "I think" part in there, when that reporter gets up there.

Student: Yes.

Mrs. Glenda: Does he or she say, you know I thought or we thought that this was gonna happen.

Student: Um hum.

Mrs. Glenda: Is the why in there, well we thought that is was gonna happen because of the distance weight whatever, ok then the next role will be summarizing findings and results, you're listening, did they do that? did they give you the main idea of what happened? did they give it to you in order, you know we put the weights in and dah dah dah dah dat happened all right, also remember we said we don't want the who cares stuff in there so if they start telling you about their shoelace [some kids laugh] or somebody's [inaudible], you might want to remind them that that's not appropriate for the explanation, ok and the third step, and I think that this is probably the hardest step, is relating your predictions and theories to your findings, what that means is, is when you were done with the second step and you had these results, what were your results in comparison to your first steps? did your results support your first steps or did it not support it? and what that really means is, did it happen the way you thought it was gonna happen or not and then why, ok so if your, everyone's holding a card and when it's your turn to be listening for that part.

Raul: I don't have a card.

Mrs. Glenda: And you don't, oh Raul it's cuz you're up first [as reporter – Raul laughs], and when you don't hear that, I want you to try and ask the questions, now I'm sitting here and I'm sitting this way so I can

help you ask the questions, but I'm gonna look and
see first if you can come up with a question that
can get the reporter to explain more, ok, before
we start is there anybody that thinks they would
like to come up with one way a nice way of asking
a question or do you think we can just do it?

Mrs. Glenda clearly marked expectations for student conduct
and reasoning in this introduction. When reporters came up to the
front of the room the rest of the students were told that they were
not to "go on snooze control" as they may have done with their
regular science instruction. Mrs. Glenda calls attention to their
assigned intellectual roles, what she calls their "jobs." She explained
that in their new jobs as audience members they would ask questions
that corresponded to the cognitive tools they used during their
small-group investigations: predicting and theorizing, summarizing
results, and relating predictions, theories, and results. She also
defined her own role as one of waiting to see if the students could
ask questions of reporters and then supporting them if they needed
assistance. The students said very little during this discussion. When
she was finished, she called on Tammy.

Tammy:	But do we go up right there [to ask questions]?
Mrs. Glenda:	No you just put your hand up and ask the question, and remember one thing, **this is the first time, yes this is hard, the hardest job is not the reporter's job, the hardest job is all of our jobs here** [someone laughs] so that we can get a good explanation, **we're gonna construct an explanation all together,** ok? Raul you're up.
Raul:	Oh no [said in a playful, high-pitched voice].

Tammy's questions made it painfully clear that this was a whole
new world for the students where one did not even know where
to place her body to complete the jobs the Mrs. Glenda discussed.
Mrs. Glenda responded with the information she requested but also
explicitly respected the difficulty of the task set before the students
and acknowledged that everyone had a hard job as they went into

this first report where audience members would be asked to take on their roles. She set an expectation of working "all together" to achieve their common goal. Raul then reported with Qing about a pan balance problem they completed with 40 grams in the right pan and 39 grams in the left (see Investigation #4, p. 36). Steven and Emma were their other group members. All other students were assigned their "jobs" as audience members.

Raul:	Last time when we had done a game of balancing the weights, I we didn't write down how much each weight weighed so [Mrs. Glenda hands the activity card to Qing and Steven to hold up] we had to do the game over again, and (pause) we we wrote like the scores on our paper and stuff, like who won, and I wrote like I said I think that it will balance like when, what's your name [Raul looks and points at Steven].
Qing:	Steven.
Raul:	Steven um picked out some weight it was 39 weights and we couldn't match his exact weights so we put 40 weights and I said it was gonna balance because they were two very close numbers but it didn't balance, um.
Steven:	I said it was gonna balance too.
Raul:	For the second.
Mrs. Glenda:	Ok, why don't I stop you right here, who um Rosie, you have the [intellectual audience role] card that says predicting and theorizing.
Rosie:	Yup.
Mrs. Glenda:	Did you understand Raul's prediction and his theory?
Rosie:	Well . . .
Mrs. Glenda:	If you did tell me.
Rosie:	Just a little bit because he says that he thought that it will balance.
Mrs. Glenda:	Um hum.

Rosie:	Because they were two closest numbers and then it didn't balance, I know why it didn't balance because maybe it, for example if we put one forty grams on number five and 30 grams on number six, which one it will balance I don't even know.
Mrs. Glenda:	But did you did you understand his prediction, you heard the I think part, you heard that?
Rosie:	Well…
Mrs. Glenda:	Or do you think he could say it a little bit, do you think the group could say it a little bit better? Raul I'm not hangin' you out to dry, you're the first guy up here you've got the hardest job.
Rosie:	I don't remember.
Mrs. Glenda:	You don't remember, ok who had that part here, Olivia was supposed to be doing this and Carson was supposed to be doing this, and…
Steven:	Carson's sick.
Mrs. Glenda:	And neither one of them are here right now.
Steven:	Carson's sick, that's why.
Mrs. Glenda:	Would it be all right if I took on this role?
Student:	Yeah.
Student:	Yeah.
Mrs. Glenda:	It would be all right?
Student:	Yeah.
Student:	Yeah.
Mrs. Glenda:	Well then I'm going to say Raul could you please read me just the prediction?
Raul:	I think that it will balance the first number, you see I said I think it will balance and I was explaining why I thought it was gonna balance, and ok [Qing points to Raul's notebook and whispers something to him].
Mrs. Glenda:	Ok ok and Qing is telling me that that was the prediction right there, right?

Raul:	Um hum.
Qing:	And then he was telling why.
Mrs. Glenda:	And why is the what?
Raul:	Why is the ...
Qing:	Balance.
Mrs. Glenda:	The theory?
Raul:	Yeah.
Mrs. Glenda:	Theory, ok, so it is there.

This interaction demonstrated just how difficult it was for the students to take on these new roles as questioners of one another. Although Rosie was able to restate Raul's prediction and theory clearly, her next impulse was to offer a report of a balance scale problem that may not balance, based on her own experience that day. This was an important intellectual move to find a parallel problem that provided the same results as the one the reporters were presenting – uncertainty about the result. However, when explicitly questioned by Mrs. Glenda to evaluate if she heard the "I think part" in Raul's report, Rosie struggled and could not answer. Stepping into a role where one student must understand another student's ideas and be able to express those ideas to others was challenging. Rosie could repeat what Raul said and provide a parallel problem from her experiences. However, she could not evaluate if what Raul said was a prediction, a theory, or something else. To do this required coordinating new vocabulary such as prediction and theory with new practices such as actively listening to peers and using metacognitive reflection to determine if desired features were present and understood. Prompting students to actively listen to each other and to think about their own thinking is not typical in most classrooms. Therefore, there were many things that Rosie needed to coordinate to answer Mrs. Glenda's questions, things that she had not necessarily done in the past. Mrs. Glenda asked if she could take on this role when students who were assigned to do it were not available to do so. She modeled how she would go about checking her own understanding of Raul's prediction and theory. Raul and Qing participated with Mrs. Glenda to identify the prediction and the theory. Linking these new terms to practices was a large part of these first few days of instruction.

Mrs. Glenda then turned to the students in the audience again, asking who had the next role, summarizing findings and results. Denise and Dai raised their hands but were unsure of how to proceed.

Mrs. Glenda:	Ok, do you have any questions for Raul [Denise shakes her head no] did he summarize his findings? Can you repeat them? [Denise shakes her head no and one child giggles a little] Dai can you repeat his findings or his results? [Dai shakes his head no] no, what more would you need to know?
Dai:	I don't know.
Mrs. Glenda:	Do you want him to read it again? [Denise shakes her head yes]
Dai:	Sure.
Mrs. Glenda:	Ok, let's have him read it again and then you guys listen.
Raul:	What part do you want?
Mrs. Glenda:	Well you just gave your theory, your prediction and your theory.
Raul:	Ok.
Mrs. Glenda:	Ok.
Raul:	The first number was 39 grams that was what Steven picked and since there wasn't um exactly 39 more that we could like put together to make 39, so we had ta use one higher so we used 40 grams and I didn't exactly think it was gonna balance but because it was two close numbers I said it was gonna balance.
Steven:	It barely did.
Raul:	Yeah it almost balanced it was very close but it didn't balance.
Mrs. Glenda:	Ok.
Denise:	I'm thinking.

Mrs. Glenda:	You're thinking (pause) did you understand what Raul said? Could you try to explain to us what he said?
Denise:	Say the whole thing over again?
Mrs. Glenda:	Say it the way you understood it.
Denise:	[inaudible] say it?
Mrs. Glenda:	Yeah, just the way you can say it.
Denise:	That he used one more gram than he was supposed to, and I have a question. So do you think that made a difference?
Raul:	Yep, that one little gram was heavier than the 39 so it made it go down it wouldn't balance, cuz that number's higher, 40.
Mrs. Glenda:	Ok, now, if you're, put your hand down because you guys have different roles, Dai did you understand?

Denise and Dai struggled to come up with questions for the reporters when their turn came to ask about the results. The students communicated at first only through gesture, shaking their heads "no" to each of the Mrs. Glenda's queries. They eventually agreed with the Mrs. Glenda's suggestion to ask Raul to read his report again. Once he finished, Denise remarked that she was thinking. Mrs. Glenda paused to give her time to think and prepare to speak. When she did not speak, Mrs. Glenda entered to support her to articulate what she had just heard, "could you try to explain to us what he said?" Denise seemed puzzled by this request and asked for clarification about Mrs. Glenda's request over several turns. Denise expressed what Rosie might have been feeling in the first transcript example (see pages 61–62). Mrs. Glenda's request to repeat another students' findings in her own words was unusual and she seemed surprised that she was being asked to do this. Eventually she did provide a summary and then went on to ask an important question. After this, Mrs. Glenda worked with Dai for about 5 minutes to ensure that he understood the result (this is not shown here.) At the end of this time, it was still unclear if he understood. He asked one question about method, "Raul, what you guys did?" This question was repeated based on a model Mrs. Glenda provided. Dai was never able to restate what the group found out in his own words.

At this point, Mrs. Glenda noticed that they only had 9 minutes left, so even though she was not certain if Dai understood, she quickly transitioned to working with students who had the third audience role, checking relationships between predictions, theories, and results. Christie and Tammy were assigned that role.

Tammy:	What does that mean?
Mrs. Glenda:	What your results had to do with your original prediction.
Raul:	I'll just try to say this, I said I think it'll balance because the weights were close and we found that they nearly balanced but one was just a little bit lower, they were very close but just one was just a little bit lower, because it was the 40 because it was a gram heavier.
Mrs. Glenda:	Are you clear? [shaking head no] What do you need to know to...
Tammy:	I'm confused.
Mrs. Glenda:	You're confused, ok and you know something it's ok to ask somebody it's ok to say I'm confused, could you explain that to me again, or do you have a specific question like...
Tammy:	I don't know any questions yet.
Mrs. Glenda:	You don't know any questions yet, I know this is hard, um, ok do you know which part you're confused about or are you confused about the whole thing?
Tammy:	The whole thing.
Mrs. Glenda:	The whole thing, ok lets break it up into parts, um did you hear did you hear him compare his results to his prediction? did you hear that?
Tammy:	Kinda.
Mrs. Glenda:	Kinda, did you hear it well or not too well?

Tammy:	Not too well.
Mrs. Glenda:	That might be your first question is, Raul can you can you compare for me your results to your original prediction?
Tammy:	Can you compare your resights [self corrects] results to the original condition?
Raul:	Ok, well you see I said I think it would balance because of the close numbers and then the results were that it nearly balanced not that it actually balanced, it was close but, that one little gram [shakes his finger at the page of his notebook and changes his intonation slightly when he says one little gram].
Mrs. Glenda:	Does that make it more clear for you?
Tammy:	Well not really much to ask a question about.
Mrs. Glenda:	There's not much to ask questions on? no, Christie how about you do you have a question for them?
Christie:	What side was the one that went down like a tiny bit?
Raul:	40 went lower than 39 because it was a gram heavier.
Christie:	But what side right or left?
Raul:	Um, it was the right, and if you notice, if you look on this thing it looks like it's bending already even though there's nothing on it.
Mrs. Glenda:	So we're not even sure if this is calibrated exactly.
Raul:	Not exactly.
Mrs. Glenda:	Not exactly.
Raul:	I mean who knows.
Mrs. Glenda:	Who knows?
Denise:	Maybe it has a piece of hair in it.
Mrs. Glenda:	So what do you guys think of this for an explanation, do you all understand this?

Tammy articulated what all the students seemed to be experiencing – confusion. She did not know where to stand (at the beginning of the lesson), or what to ask (at this point in the lesson). The confusion had consequences for content, epistemology, and students' self-evaluations of competence. Mrs. Glenda supported Tammy's statement and remarked that it was okay to be confused and to ask for clarification from others. This statement explicitly challenged the traditional background assumptions about school. The students believed that "being right" was essential and "being confused" was problematic. Mrs. Glenda wanted the students to understand that being confused was just fine and that asking for clarification was an important part of having a productive conversation in school science. When Tammy said she did not have any specific questions, Mrs. Glenda modeled one and Tammy posed it to Raul. Once Raul responded, Tammy proclaimed, "well, not really much to ask a question about" because Raul had clearly articulated the relationship between prediction, theory, and results. Mrs. Glenda repeated Tammy's proclamation and then moved on to the next student assigned this role, Christie. Christie had formulated a question but the question she asked was not a high-quality, content-focused question, it was about whether the right or the left side of the balance went down. This question, however, did lead to an important discussion about calibrating the scale with some students questioning whether or not it was done properly. Denise suggested that perhaps even a small piece of hair was in the pan balance and that could have affected the results. At the end of this discussion (following the transcript above), Mrs. Glenda asked the students if they understood now. They indicated that they did, so she asked for a volunteer to do the "really hard thing" of summarizing what they learned about all three ways of thinking like a scientist (or steps, as she referred to them). The students were unable to do this. However they had articulated their confusions and concerns in a way that was beginning to be more understandable to each other and to Mrs. Glenda. The lesson ended with the students and Mrs. Glenda discussing what was difficult about this process.

> *Mrs. Glenda:*   Ok you know what for the first one of these things
>   you guys were incredible, absolutely incredible,

	how many of you think that the first step, the predicting and theory part is pretty easy [Mrs. Glenda raises her hand and kids begin to raise their hands] is it pretty easy to give a prediction.
Raul:	Uh huh yeah.
Mrs. Glenda:	I thought this was gonna happen, does it get harder as we go along through it?
Raul:	Um hum yeah a little bit.
Mrs. Glenda:	A little bit.
Rosie:	Well the first time it's not easy but [overlapping speech with Steven].
Steven:	[overlapping speech with Rosie] The third part's hard.
Mrs. Glenda:	The third part's very hard it's even hard for me to try to say it in ways that I can really talk to you.
Rosie:	The first time, we, it's hard to do because we don't understand very well what we're doing.
Mrs. Glenda:	Right.
Rosie:	By the next time you understand it.

Mrs. Glenda ended on an encouraging and positive note, even though it was a challenging day for her and for the students. Mrs. Glenda had some predictions about what was likely to be difficult and she used her own ideas to question the students at the end of the session about their experiences. The students may have been less clear about their difficulties but followed along with Mrs. Glenda's suggestions. They definitely thought the first time through had not been easy. Steven commented that the "third part" or relating findings back to original predictions and theories was very hard. Mrs. Glenda concurred and said she even struggled to come up with effective ways to talk about this with the students. Rosie ended the session on an upbeat note, remarking that the first time is hard because you don't understand it but "by the next time you understand it."

Many things happened on this first day of reporting out. First, it was clear that this process of using intellectual audience roles and questioning each other about predictions, theories, and results was entirely new to the students. On a basic level, they did not know Mrs. Glenda or one another (thus Raul had to ask Steven his name even though they were in the same group), they did not know how to physically arrange themselves in the classroom (thus Tammy asked where she should position herself in the classroom when taking on the audience roles), and they were puzzled by Mrs. Glenda's repeated requests for audience members to restate or repeat what the reporter said in their own words. In some cases, students did not know what to ask questions about and in others they had difficulty forming questions. When they did succeed in asking questions they often did so by accepting and repeating Mrs. Glenda's model. Denise and Christie asked their own questions, but it was largely ceremonial in nature (asking a question because Mrs. Glenda told them to) and not because they really wanted to know the reporters' responses. There was a general swirl of confusion with Mrs. Glenda's explicit acknowledgement that this was difficult work but that they were going to do it together. The students demonstrated trust in Mrs. Glenda and the process. No one refused to participate, although there were times when the students' reluctance and reticence was keenly felt. Denise, Dai, Tammy, and Christie all asked questions. Raul repeatedly read sections of his report for the group. Steven shared what he thought was hard about the day and Rosie commented that she thought next time they would understand better, that things are always hard the first time through.

In her reflections on the day, Mrs. Glenda commented that the first step, especially the focus on predictions, was a strength for the group. However, the students' did not seem to understand the two other ways of knowing in science.

Mrs. Glenda: The next two steps are not natural steps for them. I mean, it's just not there when I went around. I think we're gonna hafta focus one step at a time. And, I sometimes think, it's not that you're fighting F/OD but it's so much a part of the way they do science. You are butting up against [cuts herself off] even Denise said to me, this isn't science.

Just as she had done on the baseline day, Mrs. Glenda recognized the limitations in the students' reasoning practices. She suggested that she and Leslie were going to have to focus "one step at a time" while the students were learning more about these new ways of knowing. She also commented that the students were comparing what they were doing in our experimental classroom with their regular classroom science. Because it was different, the students' assessment was that Mrs. Glenda was "not doing science." There was initial resistance to this new approach to science and a confusion about what they were doing and why. Next, Mrs. Glenda stated, in the quote below, that the focus on the ways of knowing was going to have to take a back seat to the "group process" which in her mind had to come first.

> *Mrs. Glenda:*   I tried to write last night in my journal after I was talking to you on the phone and the best way I could come up with this was um I feel like we're getting the group process at this point, just a big group process and then each child is an individual who has a zillion little individual components and those are gonna come out but the time constraints and the getting to know each other factor, I hafta go with the group process to start and then let the other part come through. I know I've definitely got the notions of who is who and who needs what from me. I have notions about who doesn't need me at all and I think that's pretty obvious by who I stayed away from.

Mrs. Glenda reflected on the importance of establishing the group as a classroom community, "a big group process" of "getting to know you" first and then allowing the individual children and their "zillion little individual components" to come through. She worried again about the time constraints because there would be only 12 sessions with the students. She also indicated that she felt confident that she was getting a good sense of what each student needed and that she was using this to make decisions about how to allocate her teaching time.

***Day 3: "See, I really believe that all this stuff is really in there,
it's just asking the right questions to make sure it all comes out."*** On
Day 3, Mrs. Glenda began the reporting session once again under
significant time pressure.

Mrs. Glenda: Excuse me ladies and gentlemen, excuse me excuse
me, [inaudible], I'm gonna let group C [many
kids are still coming in and getting settled] ok
first because they haven't had a chance to report
yet and realistically excuse me realistically I think
that's all we'll get to because we have to go to
lunch, before group C gets up here I need give out
jobs, Raul, you have step three relating predictions, theories, and findings, Emma you have step
one you hafta make sure that there is a prediction
and a theory, Qing you have step 2 make sure that
they do summarizing their result, Steven, where is
Steven?

Steven: I have step 3.

Mrs. Glenda: You've got step 3, did you know that, ok great,
Rosie you've got step one prediction and theory,
Rich you have step 2 make sure that you hear
a summary of results, Tammy you've got step
3 relating theory, prediction, and findings, and
Olivia you've got step one, prediction and theory,
ok, you make sure you hear the we guessed and we
thought and then why.

Olivia: Why they guessed that?

Mrs. Glenda: Why they guessed that. Excuse me, last call, we
now have 9 minutes and I wanna get this done,
Denise right up here, I will hold this for you guys
and I will stand way back here [Mrs. Glenda stands
behind the chart stand holding up the group's dia-
gram] and you know what I'm hoping for, I am
absolutely positively hoping that you don't hear
my voice anymore, so everybody has a role.

Student:	Yup.
Mrs. Glenda:	Everybody knows what they're supposed to do, let's see you do it.

In this excerpt, Mrs. Glenda made it clear that they were rushed for time, that the students had their role assignments, and that she was hoping that they would be the ones to speak from that point forward. That was not exactly what happened, however, as the interaction continued. Carson and Christie were reporting for their group about a pan balance problem with 45 grams in the right pan and 20 grams in the left. Dai and Denise were their other group members assigned to be scribes (see Investigation #4, p. 36).

Carson:	I don't even know what I'm supposed to do.
Mrs. Glenda:	That's ok because you've got all these 10 other people in the room who are gonna help you, Carson come on up, Christie come on up [Mrs. Glenda whispers to them to let them know what they should do].
Rosie:	Mrs. Glenda, can you do [inaudible] [Mrs. Glenda gestures to Rosie to be quiet by putting her finger to her mouth].
Mrs. Glenda:	[Mrs. Glenda quiets Steven and then there is a long pause in conversation. Carson stands with his head facing the floor.] Carson, can I ask you a question? Since it feels to me like maybe you guys didn't have enough time to get a good three-step explanation in place.
Carson:	We didn't even know what to do.
Mrs. Glenda:	Would it help if people just started right away to ask questions?
Denise:	I could help Carson.
Mrs. Glenda:	Ok ok but Denise but it's not your job to help for this thing, prediction and theory people this is your job now let's see if you can get a prediction from Carson and a theory, go ahead.

As Carson and Christie stood before the rest of the class, it was quickly clear that they did not know how to proceed. Mrs. Glenda remarked that it was okay not to know how to begin and that there were 10 other people in the room (the students in the audience) who were there to help him. She positioned Carson and Christie up front and whispered support and direction. Then as Carson continued to stand silently looking at the ground, Mrs. Glenda suggested that perhaps the audience should start asking questions related to their roles. In the midst of this, Denise, Carson's group member, offered to help him. This would be a typical practice in most classroom settings, to allow a fellow group member to help a student who needed it. But, in this case, Mrs. Glenda was very clear that it was not Denise's job to help, it was the audience's job to do that by asking Carson questions that would draw out predictions, theories, summaries of results, and relationships among them. This placed value on a particular practice of having the audience engage with the reporters. Implied in this value was the desire to have conversations take place across students in different groups that were working on different focal activities. It also affirmed that the reporters had a job to do and that the rest of the community members were there to make sure that the reporters succeeded in doing it. There were high expectations for every student to adopt every role and plenty of support to make that possible. Mrs. Glenda viewed Carson as having more difficulties expressing his strong intuitive thinking. She wanted to position him to develop the sense of confidence and competence that he lacked. The conversation continued and the students in the audience began asking Carson for more information about his group's activity.

Olivia:	How many grams does he hafta put in?
Student:	On each side.
Raul:	How many are you putting on each side?
Rosie:	How many grams do you put on this one and how many grams do you put on this one?
Carson:	I don't know [looking down at the floor].

Olivia, Raul, and Rosie jumped right in to ask Carson how much weight he and his group placed in each side of the pan balance.

Carson could not remember or did not know. He was clearly struggling and looked uncomfortable as he stood up in front of the class with his eyes facing the floor. Mrs. Glenda decided to ask Carson's reporting partner, Christie, to see if she could help him.

Mrs. Glenda:	Christie do you know how many grams you guys were working with?
Dai:	It's about 37.
Rich:	It's right there.
Dai:	We just put all of them in.
Denise:	[consults her lab notebook] This one has 20 in it and this one has 45, yeah 45.

Christie did not respond but several other children commented. Denise, as the scribe in the group who had initially been told to wait for audience members to ask questions, consulted her laboratory notebook to report this information to the class. Then Mrs. Glenda entered the conversation to prompt students to think about predictions and theories.

Mrs. Glenda:	Prediction people, are you satisfied did you hear a prediction?
Student:	No.
Raul:	No, no prediction.
Mrs Glenda:	What did you hear?
Raul:	All she said was that [overlapping speech with Denise] she put 20 on one side and 45 on the other.
Denise:	[overlapping speech with Raul] It's not my report, I'm the scribe, it's Carson's report.
Mrs. Glenda:	Denise, Denise.
Raul:	So what do you think is gonna come down, and why do you think it's gonna come down, what side?
Denise:	I think the right.
Mrs. Glenda:	You know right? [said to Carson].

Denise:	Right's gonna go down.
Mrs. Glenda:	Denise, Denise it's his job and I just heard him say I don't think I know, go ahead [Carson].
Carson:	I think that the 45 in that and the 20 in that that that'll go down because there's more weight in it.
Raul:	Ok.

In this segment, Raul claimed that he did not hear any prediction. He said he just heard Denise's statement of how much weight was on each side. Denise got defensive about Raul's comment and claimed that it was not her fault that Raul did not know this because it was Carson's responsibility to report. Mrs. Glenda directly addressed Denise because she was already concerned that Carson did not feel like he could productively contribute as the reporter. Mrs. Glenda's intention was to support Carson to feel successful in this role with the help of the audience, so Denise's blame did not support her intended emotional climate in the classroom. Raul then prompted the reporters with a remarkably clear question about their prediction. Denise jumped in to answer. Mrs. Glenda directly chastised her and insisted, just as Denise did a few moments earlier, that this was Carson's job and she heard him give a response. This opened the floor to Carson who spoke for the first time since he said, "I don't know" to earlier questions. He was able to communicate both his prediction and his theory. Mrs. Glenda followed Carson's comment by checking in with Raul, who had been assigned the role of checking predictions and theories, to see if he was satisfied.

Mrs. Glenda:	Did you hear a prediction?
Raul:	Yeah, I heard a prediction.
Mrs. Glenda:	And did you hear a theory too?
Raul:	Yup.
Mrs. Glenda:	Prediction and theory people are you satisfied?
Student:	Yeah.
Raul:	I'm satisfied, yup.

Raul confirmed that he was satisfied with what he had heard. Within this stretch of interaction, beginning with Carson and Christie struggling to report and ending with Raul confirming his satisfaction, certain values and practices began to emerge for a second time around in the classroom context. Working with Carson, Mrs. Glenda reiterated valuable ways of being that had come up on Day 2: Being a person who did not know how to get started was okay, being a person who needed help from others was okay, and being an audience member meant asking questions to help reporters articulate their ideas. There were some ways of being that were discouraged. Being a person who talked for others was only okay under certain circumstances. Being a person who blamed others for shortcomings in a report was not okay. These ways of being were not named. There were no mini-lectures or charts. Instead, they were embedded in interactional practices that Mrs. Glenda was working to recalibrate in the classroom.

During the latter part of Carson and Christie's report several students played crucial supporting roles in the process of learning how to ask questions of reporters. The students continued struggling with the last step – asking questions about the relationship between the prediction, theory, and results. Tammy and Steven had been assigned the role of questioning the reporters about this issue.

Mrs. Glenda:	. . . do you remember last [time] Tammy, you and I did it one step at a time, do you remember how we did it [asked questions]? Ok, look at me [Tammy is looking at the floor], it's it's this is this is hard, do you remember what their theory is?
Tammy:	No.
Rich:	Yes.
Mrs. Glenda:	Do you remember what their theory is? Does anybody in the group remember what kind of theory we're dealing with? What kind of theory are we dealing with?
Rich:	That there's more weight on one side.

Mrs. Glenda supported Tammy, reminding her of the last time they worked together to ask questions of reporters. She validated that it was hard work to ask these questions. She also validated Tammy, asking her to look up at her rather than looking down at the floor. Through her own facial expressions and body posture, leaning in toward Tammy, she wanted to convey that she understood and was there to support her. She opened up the conversation to other students and Rich came to the fore, reminding the group of the theory that had just been presented. Once Mrs. Glenda had Rich's response in hand, she continued to scaffold the experience of asking questions.

Mrs. Glenda:	Ok, we're dealing with a weight theory, ok, Tammy, from the very beginning they thought that because there was more weight it was gonna come down, ok, then they did, Carson, when you did your experiment, the side with the most weight went down. [shakes head yes] All you hafta get them to do is make the c [interrupts herself], did they think what was gonna happen happen and why? That's it, so you might wanna say like Carson, in the beginning you thought that the side with more weight was gonna go down is that really what happened? That's it, it's as simple as that. Did you think what was gonna happen really happened?
Tammy:	Did you think what was gonna happen really happened? [Carson nods yes]
Mrs. Glenda:	Really, Steven, I need you to ask them the question, Carson's already said what he thought, what was gonna happen really happened, now you need to ask him the why part.
Raul:	Just say why did it happen.
Mrs. Glenda:	Do you understand what I'm asking you to do? Not really, huh?
Raul:	Just say why did it happen? Just ask him why did it happen, why do you think. [Mrs. Glenda interrupts him]

Mrs. Glenda:	Ok, even if somebody who doesn't have this job, if somebody else who doesn't have this job wants to try to ask Carson a question, Raul, go ahead.
Raul:	Why do you think what happened happened?
Carson:	Because there's more weight on one side than the other.
Mrs. Glenda:	Ok, Rich, you have another question for them, go ahead.
Rich:	Just because there's more weight on one side, why do you think it's gonna go down?
Denise:	Cuz.
Carson:	Because both of the buckets were [inaudible].
Denise:	Because there was 45 grams and 20 grams, I don't think it would be even.
Carson:	Yeah.
Denise:	Or I don't think the left would go down.

After Tammy repeated Mrs. Glenda's suggested words, Mrs. Glenda turned to Steven, who also shared responsibility for this audience role. Steven did not understand what Mrs. Glenda was asking him to do. Experiencing difficulty with this new way of being was once again validated and supported in this context both with Tammy and Steven. Mrs. Glenda made it clear that everyone was working together to figure out how to be a person who asks questions about other students' predictions, theories, results, and the relationship between them. Mrs. Glenda decided to open the floor to other students who were not assigned this role as it was evident that other students were prepared to do so. Raul, who had been trying to coach Steven, opted in to the conversation and asked a question, "why do you think what happened happened?" Carson responded saying that there was more weight on one side than the other. Rich followed, building on Raul's question, but pushing for more of an explanation – in essence asking why weight matters. He said, "just because there's more weight on one side why do think it's gonna go down?" Denise, in a move that is a first for the students, told Rich why they did not choose the other possible alternatives – that the scale would balance or that the left side would go down. This did not exactly address Rich's question about why weight was important, but she explained the process they used to eliminate the other options. Mrs. Glenda did not stop these exchanges even though Denise was not the reporter. She had supported the reporters throughout to take up their roles but also wanted to foster discussion about the third step, which proved difficult for most of the students. She wanted peer models with "kid talk" to come to the fore. Many different issues were weighed against one another in these moment-to-moment interactions. Juggling all these competing demands at once was the hallmark of Mrs. Glenda's teaching that embodied a deep wisdom in practice.

This was a crucial turning point for all subsequent conversations. Until this moment, with the exception of one case, Mrs. Glenda had been responsible for initiating all discussions that prompted students to coordinate their predictions and theories with their evidence. However, after this point, the students initiated all but two instances of coordinating predictions and theories with evidence. In these interactions then, there was a "passing of the baton" from Mrs. Glenda to the students. Mrs. Glenda marked this event and Tammy and Olivia discussed a practice that they used that then became a tool for the entire classroom.

Mrs. Glenda:	Do you guys understand, do you think your questions helped you to understand?
Student:	Yes.
Mrs. Glenda:	Do you think like because Rich could ask a question that could make Denise say what she already knew was there, **see I really believe that all this stuff is really in there, it's just asking the right questions to make sure it all comes out.**
Tammy:	I wrote down some of the questions, the one she asked and . . .
Mrs. Glenda:	That's really cool.
Olivia:	Me too.

Mrs. Glenda: So does it help, this is a really good question to ask, does it help if you hear somebody else ask a question in a way that you know you could ask it, does it help to write those down? Would it help if we made a big chart, if Leslie and I sat and copied some of those questions down and just put them up somewhere so that you could use those questions?

Asking the right questions to "make sure it all comes out" was a way of being that was enacted and valued in this episode. This was an important breakthrough for the class. Tammy and Olivia wrote down questions and told Mrs. Glenda about this practice. This was another significant turning point that Mrs. Glenda was able to immediately value and build on. She suggested that she and Leslie work to create a list of questions for the students based on things they asked to date. Mrs. Glenda picked up on this at the beginning of Day 5 when she engaged the class in building the "questions chart" (discussed later in this chapter).

Mrs. Glenda reflected on what happened during Day 3, commenting on how hard it was to transform the students' passive stance toward their roles as audience members. During reporting the students were allowed to help themselves to pretzels as a snack since they missed their regular classroom snack time. Mrs. Glenda observed how this snack became a clue to one student's "zoning out."

Mrs. Glenda: It's so hard for them in so many ways because you can tell they're used to tuning out. They are used to this sort of passive report where someone else is doing the work and I can put my pretzels over my eyes and just kinda zone out. And it's really hard for them to understand that this is active participation all the way through it. You have roles in the audience and at this stage they're more important than the reporter's role.

The students in the early days of the study continued to struggle to shift their roles during reporting. Some students seemed to move back and forth between engaged listening and participation and "zoning out." For Mrs. Glenda, it was important to recognize that this was to be expected and that we were asking a lot of the students. They were beginning to take up these new roles. In addition to reflecting on the students behavior, she also reflected on her own, clearly articulating what she thought she need to change to support the students taking on more active, participatory roles.

> *Mrs. Glenda:* My own behavior, I hafta modify a little bit. I hafta stop making this sound so official and get it back into kids words. Cuz Tammy was trying to spit out exactly what I said [laughs] and that was one of the questions I wrote to you in my journal. What would this look like in the beginning? Would they like take my model as the truth or would they be able to generalize? But I'm sure a couple days into this and they'll be generalizing.... I'm not clear on the third step at all and that's why Tammy was wrestling with it so I need some kid talk for the third step.

Mrs. Glenda wanted to return to using what she called "kid language" to ensure that students would be able to take up more participatory roles during reporting. To do that, she needed to clarify her own thinking, especially about the third step of relating findings back to original predictions and theories that the class had struggled with now for two days. Furthermore, she needed to be sure that she was modeling the use of these new ways of knowing and doing using language that the students would be able to understand and take up effectively. She also wondered aloud how the initial models that she presented might be repeated at first but then modified over time (what she called "generalized") by the students.

Mrs. Glenda also reflected on her ability to get the students to articulate theories, which seemed much harder to surface than predictions.

> *Mrs. Glenda:* They were fixated on certainly the predicting part but for Tammy especially she was pretty accurate about her predictions and her results, I mean she

wasn't predicting incorrectly at all so she had to have some little working theory there which obviously I wasn't getting her to articulate but I think we could probably get that.

Mrs. Glenda noted that she needed to find a way to get the students to surface their "little working theories" in more effective ways and that this was something that she could do. She and Leslie talked about designing an introductory lesson to support students to understand, explicitly label, and discuss their theories. On Day 4, this is how the lesson began, with Mrs. Glenda working with the students to reflect on a report she created. She asked them to find the prediction, theory, results, and the relationship between them.

Day 4: "Let's see if we can work this through..." Before the students began their work on Day 4, Mrs. Glenda brought them together to focus on an explanation that she had written on chart paper. The explanation was written after completing a balance scale problem with two 10-gram weights on number 3 on the left and one 10-gram weight on number 1 on the right (see Investigation #3, p. 36 for a similar problem that varies both weight and distance from the fulcrum). Mrs. Glenda explained what she wanted the students to do:

Mrs. Glenda: What I've done this afternoon is I've put an activity up on the chart here [points to chart paper] and I've written an explanation. And what I need to have happen, I'll read it to you and I won't assign roles right now so anybody can answer questions for me. But as I read it through, I want you to listen for a prediction, a theory, the results, and then the third step where we go back and see if our results support our theory. Ok this is the explanation [begins to read from the chart] I think that the 2 ten grams on the left is going to go down and not the 1 ten gram because it's only 10 grams. That's what I think. Do you know the answer? I don't know if you know the answer but I do.

Raul: Who wrote that?

Mrs. Glenda:	I did.
Raul:	I know the answer.
Mrs. Glenda:	**Ok let's see if we can work this through.** Can anybody find the prediction up here? Qing.

Mrs. Glenda opened this exercise by asking for something she believed that the students were able to easily provide – an assessment of the prediction. Several students participated as they identified the prediction – or the "I think part." Then, Mrs. Glenda moved on to one issue she felt was tripping them up – the theory.

Mrs. Glenda:	Ok, does anybody see, that's the prediction, does anybody see a theory?
Raul:	Um hmm.
Mrs. Glenda:	The why you think that.
Raul:	I know the theory.
Mrs. Glenda:	Yes, Dai.
Dai:	I see it [gets up to move toward the chart].
Mrs. Glenda:	Come on up. I'll give you a different color [marker to mark the theory on the chart].
Dai:	I need to sit here too [sits down in front of the chart and begins to read it].
Mrs. Glenda:	Sure, here you go [gives him the marker].
Dai:	[looking at the chart] The why?
Mrs. Glenda:	Yeah, the why you think [pause – other students are raising their hands but they do not jump in].
Dai:	Here [looks to Mrs. Glenda as he places the marker on the chart].
Mrs. Glenda:	[moves her hand to the chart as she begins to speak] Ok, starting right here at because is that where you think it is?
Dai:	No, no.
Mrs. Glenda:	It should go there? [Dai marks on the chart highlighting "that's what I think"– many students have hands raised].

Dai:	It goes here.
Mrs. Glenda:	Oh, ok, alright that's what you think. Ok, who else wants to add on?

Mrs. Glenda began the process of marking the theory by calling on a student she knew was struggling with theory building. She invited Dai to come to the chart and mark where he found the theory in the explanation. He marks the part that said, "that's what I think." Tammy followed after him to explain her idea.

Tammy:	I don't think it starts right there, I think it starts from here [places marker on the chart at "because it's only 10 grams"]
Rich:	You shouldn't use the same color [marker].
Mrs. Glenda:	That's alright.
Tammy:	Right here.
Mrs. Glenda:	Because it's only 10 grams?
Tammy:	Yeah, it's because . . .
Mrs. Glenda:	And Bin, Dai, why do I keep calling you Bin? You think that you should have that part too, "that's what I think." Ok, if I put the two of them [ideas] together is that still enough of a theory? Do you think it's enough . . .
Rich:	Yes.
Mrs. Glenda:	. . . of a theory?
Qing:	I don't think this is like why because everyone knows it's 10 grams. You need to say like why you think it. We need more.
Mrs. Glenda:	Did you guys hear that? Qing thinks that the fact that we're saying it's only 10 grams everybody already knows that. She thinks we need to be more explicit and say that the 10 grams weighs more, I mean that 20 grams weighs more than the 10 grams. Ok? And, I agree with her on that. I don't think there was enough information in there.

After Dai finished sharing his ideas, Tammy jumped right in to offer hers. She had been waiting patiently with her hand raised to share her thinking. She argued that the theory part should be the "because it's only 10 grams." Mrs. Glenda combined both Tammy and Dai's contributions and posed a question to the class, "is this enough of a theory?" Although Rich quickly blurted out that it was, Qing argued, "You need to say like why you think that. We need more." Mrs. Glenda revoiced Qing's statement and agreed with her. Asking the students to identify parts of a sample explanation and critique how effective it was at meeting their definitions of new terms and concepts like theory was a new strategy that seemed to work well to support student engagement and reflection. The students were gradually building a more complex understanding of theories and how to communicate them to others. Some students, however, continued to struggle with how to ask questions of other students during reporting time.

Day 4: "Can you say the statement and then we'll all help you turn it into a question?" During reporting on Day 4, Mrs. Glenda was trying to help Dai explain his understanding. She was holding a balance scale in her hand. Dai was concerned that having a person hold the scale rather than placing it on a table could yield unreliable results for the demonstration they were setting up together. Dai, who had difficulty asking questions over the first several days of the study, was able to articulate that he could not find a way to make his thought into a question. Mrs. Glenda took this opportunity to support Dai in making the transition from statement to question.

Dai:	I can't make it a question.
Mrs. Glenda:	It's hard, ok I'll tell you what, **can you say the statement and then we'll all help you turn it into a question**? Say what you wanna say and the rest of you guys, even though this isn't your role right now, listen to what he's gonna say and see if we can turn it into a question, go ahead.
Dai:	I only get, I only can only say the answer.
Mrs. Glenda:	Ok, then say the answer and let's see if we can turn the answer into a question, go ahead.

Dai:	Ok.
Mrs. Glenda:	Let's try this.
Dai:	I think…
Mrs. Glenda:	Rosie listen please.
Dai:	I think because the scale is because when you put it down it's more comfortable, I guess.
Raul:	It's …yeah, it's flatter.
Dai:	Yeah.
Rich:	It's more comfortable?
Raul:	You mean…
Dai:	Flatter so it's more kinda…
Qing:	It's kinda balanced.
Raul:	Yeah it's almost balanced except that one's lower.
Dai:	Yeah.
Mrs. Glenda:	But it's ok, so are you concerned that the way I had the scale…
Dai:	Yeah.
Mrs. Glenda:	…wasn't giving accurate results?
Dai:	Yeah.
Mrs. Glenda:	**So do you see what I just did for you? You said what, you said it in a sentence form, ok, and I'm asking you a question, so I want, that's exactly what I want you guys to be doing (pause) so I asked I asked him if he was concerned if it was the way I used the materials.** [a few omitted lines of transcript]
Dai:	Because I guess it was [inaudible], like it goes in your hand like this and the scale just goes turning around.
Mrs. Glenda:	Ok you did it right, you did it absolutely right, **the hardest thing to do is when you know something in your head but you're trying to get it outta somebody else's head, so you hafta take what you say and try to flip it into a question, Carson I know you're looking at me like what**

> **is she talking about but, I want you guys to do**
> **what the teacher usually does, you know how**
> **the teacher usually asks the questions.**

Student: Yeah.

Mrs. Glenda: **I don't want to be the one to ask the questions,**
> **I want you guys to ask the questions.**

In this interaction, Mrs. Glenda supported Dai and the rest of the students as they made the transition from question answerers to active listeners who ask important questions. When Dai claimed that the only thing he could say was the answer, Mrs. Glenda suggested that Dai present what he considered "the answer" and that everyone else help him transform his answer into a question. In this interchange, Mrs. Glenda made explicit the process of checking one's own understanding against the ideas of others. She suggested that when Dai turned his answer into a question, he was "knowing something in [his] own head but trying to get it outta somebody else's head." Mrs. Glenda was encouraging students to take ideas that seemed relevant to them and use these ideas as resources to pose questions of the reporters. She explicitly commented that she wanted the students to take up this kind of questioning even though students often thought of questioning as the teacher's job. This discussion also included important conceptual and linguistic context, expanding opportunities for all students to share in creating and discussing important academic language. By this time, the students had many opportunities to see Mrs. Glenda model asking questions, to experience her support as they took on the role of questioners, and to begin to get a sense of what kinds of questions they could ask in each of the audience roles. They were making connections between their own knowledge and that of others through a central way of being together in dialogue.

In her reflections on the discussion during reporting on Day 4, Mrs. Glenda continued her assessment of what students needed but also talked much more about what pedagogical approaches she might use to address students' needs. In the early reflections on Day 4, she returned to how Olivia and Tammy wrote down other students' questions on Day 3. She took up this idea of writing down students' questions as a practice of public documentation to help other students who were struggling in their audience roles.

Mrs. Glenda:	I think the first part [of the reporting that happened on Day 3] was amazing and Tammy and Olivia jotted down questions.
Leslie:	What did you think about that?
Mrs. Glenda:	Well, I thought it was great. You know it kinda, there is something about a kid being able to hook up to kid text and they hafta do that first because you can describe basically [interrupts herself] this might sound silly but if you're not somebody who can draw on or regurgitate a description, you're not gonna do it. I don't learn like that. And, that's why sometimes when I'm in the forums at the University I can't regurgitate those words. It's not that I don't know what's going on, I do. But I can't do that. So I think I know where these kids are. I think they need to know that there is this thing that is also there in their words.

When Olivia and Tammy were writing questions down they were capturing them in the students' words. This was key to Mrs. Glenda as she sought to give students access to ideas on their own terms. She compared the students' experiences to her own process of translating university forum discussions into her own more familiar language about teaching practices. She wanted to ensure that students had their own ways of speaking and thinking available, especially for steps 2 and 3 that seemed much harder for them. She thought aloud about taking this approach in the next class session together.

| *Mrs. Glenda:* | I think 3 is the hardest [step]. I think maybe what I can do is get some public stuff up there during my orientation and maybe use the ones who are struggling to ask questions and get them [questions] up there for the rest of them [students] to use. So when it's their turn or I could say to them, I know some of you are really good at step 1 and |

like doing step 1 because you know how to do it but you hafta do step 2 and step 3. So these are up for you until you figure out your own questions to ask.

In addition to thinking about creating a questions chart with the students, she worried aloud about how much to push the class. She felt uncertain about what to do to support the students and how frequently to intervene. The limited time in the study surfaced again as a concern.

Mrs. Glenda: I was just trying to figure out how to push it along, what is the right pace to push this? Or do I not push? And do I just always hafta have that faith that it's gonna happen and I don't intervene? I don't feel like that at this point. I felt like if we had just any amount of time, I'd feel different. But under this time schedule, I feel like there is intervening that should be done on my part but it's still unclear and it's gonna take me working with them [students] more, how much is enough and how much is too much? I really, I'm worried about the too much. I'm not worried about doing enough.... I just have this very deep feeling that with not even more days added, just more time everyday I could sit back and shut up very soon. My interventions would be more prompts. "Did you hear... did you hear... did you hear..." um and I don't know if that's your ultimate goal but that's my ultimate goal. I'm hoping, I mean, I think the teacher is always going to hafta be prompting for, did you hear this or did you hear that or are you satisfied but that's that. I think it's hard for these kids to shift gears. They wanna do a good job and when they're in the middle of doing a good job, you can see it on their faces.... I often know that I need to get things out publicly not

> by what they [students] said to me but by how
> someone was squirming around or by the look on
> their face, or their reaction to what somebody was
> saying.

Mrs. Glenda's ultimate goal was to occupy the role of prompting and support students' questioning of one another. With a new group of students in the limited time that she had, she was uncertain about how she should go about accomplishing this goal. She had to read the situation carefully, including picking up nonverbal cues from the students that communicated a sense of confidence and excitement in what they were doing. In addition, she had to use this reading of nonverbal cues to prompt her to "get things out publicly." She needed to respond in the moment in a way that seemed appropriate to support the students to "shift gears" and become the primary questioners. This was complex and important work and it took reflecting on ways of knowing, doing, and being in the classroom.

Day 5: Introducing the Questions Chart. "If I were sitting in the audience and my job was to be asking questions, I would kinda like some examples of some questions I could ask." After Olivia and Tammy mentioned that they were writing down questions students were asking (on Day 3), on Day 5 Mrs. Glenda decided that the students should work together to create a "Questions Chart" so that they could brainstorm ahead of time the kinds of questions one might ask in each of the audience roles. She started with questions that they had already been using during reporting sessions and placed them onto a chart labeled Questions (see Figure 3 below). This chart was described as something that was not a final draft, but something to be added to over time. It is clear from the state of the chart itself that it experienced multiple additions over time, becoming a running record of the class thinking about questioning others about central ideas related to their investigations. Mrs. Glenda placed this new valued way of being a questioner at the center of instruction and positioned the students to become competent and confident in this new practice. Using a practice of public documentation around theories (as ways of knowing) was already established as a central feature of the class. Supporting the new ways of being and knowing together

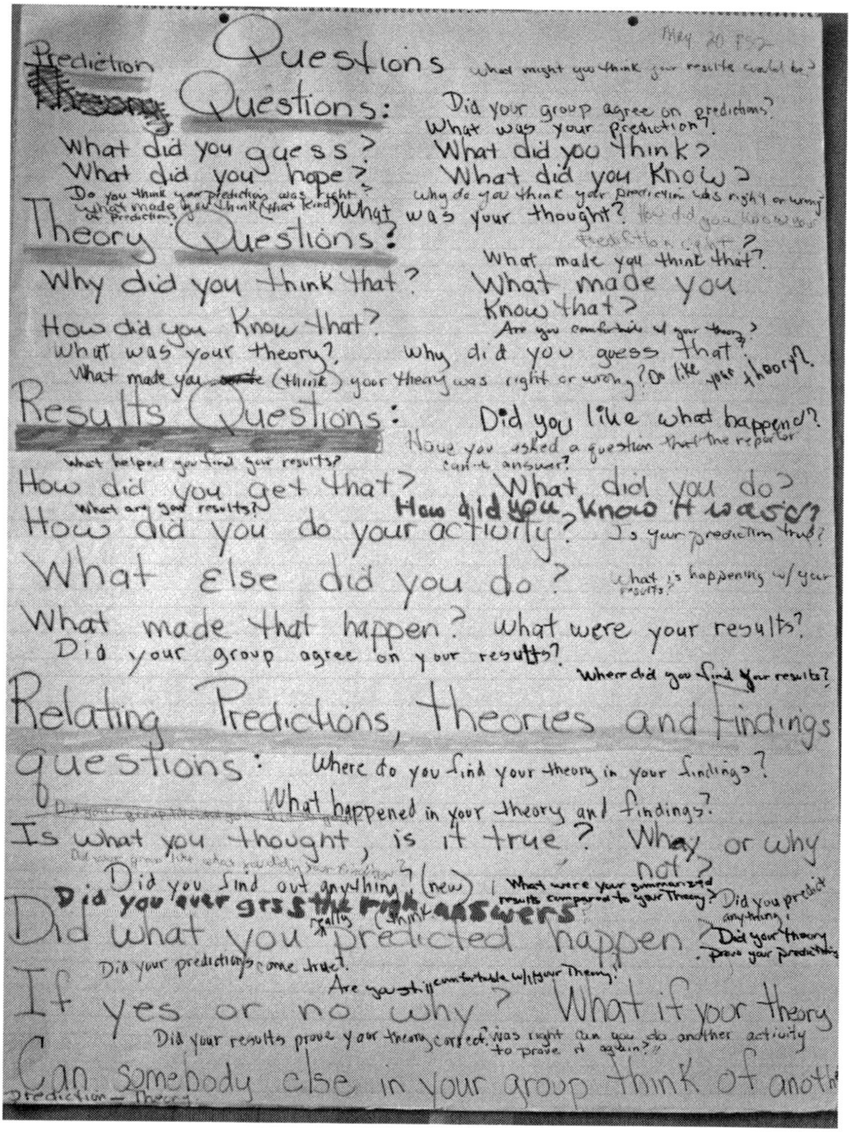

Figure 3. Questions Chart.

through initiating the development of a "Questions Chart" emerged as a result of interpersonal interaction in the classroom. The students provided the impetus and model for this work. Tammy and Olivia spontaneously began to record their questions on Day 3. The following excerpt describes how Mrs. Glenda began the discussion of the Questions Chart with the students.

Mrs. Glenda:	Um, I'm gonna do this as quietly as I can [media teacher is working and making phone calls in the room] Um I thought a lot yesterday after you guys left and **I thought about how sometimes it's really hard when you've got a job to do and you're not really sure how to do the job. Ok, I was thinking if I were sitting in the audience and my job was to be asking questions, I would kinda like some examples of some questions I could ask.** So I took the things that you guys said and tried to make up some questions and I'd like to go over these questions with you and if you can think about another way to ask these [looks at Leslie] we'll write it down, ok? [she gets a pen] Ok, for people whose job it is the check and see if predictions and theories are there, are these the kinds of questions that would help you? Like what did you guess? What did you think? What did you hope? What did you know?
Qing:	[inaudible]
Mrs. Glenda:	Oh, ok. Can I just say what was your thought?
Qing:	Yeah.
Olivia:	Yeah.
Mrs. Glenda:	[writes] Another one?
Olivia:	What was your prediction?
Mrs. Glenda:	What was your prediction? [laughs a bit] Very direct [inaudible] [writes] Ok the theory part. Why did you think that? What made you know that or think that? or How did you know that? [points to Rosie whose hand is raised]
Rosie:	Why did you guess that?
Mrs. Glenda:	Why did you guess that? [writes]

Olivia:	That's really the same thing as why did you think that.
Mrs. Glenda:	That's ok [writes while media teacher can be heard talking on the phone in the background] Anything else? [points to Olivia whose hand is raised]
Olivia:	What was your theory? [said with a big smile]
Mrs. Glenda:	What was your theory? [laughs a bit]. Olivia, you are a direct woman. I appreciate that. [writes]

Mrs. Glenda began this interaction by placing herself in the position of being asked to do this new job of questioning others about their ideas. This was an extremely important move. She directly connected her own way of being through imagining herself in the students' position of taking on this new job. Then, she validated students' work to date by writing questions from prior reporting sessions onto this beginning chart. Finally, she welcomed additions by the students, during this interaction and in future ones, asking them to think about other ways to pose questions about predictions and theories, results, and the relationship between predictions, theories, and results. Olivia, whose recording of students' questions with Tammy prompted the construction of the questions chart, played a major role in its construction. Many other students participated as well. Throughout the course of this discussion, all but one of the nine students present participated.

The students and Mrs. Glenda continued generating questions for each of the three roles. As they were nearing the end of their discussion, the students began to ask questions about what they could do with these questions.

Rich:	We can ask any one of them questions?
Mrs. Glenda:	Yes, absolutely [laughs].
Rich:	Ok, I'm gonna be asking that, that, that, that, that, that, that.
Raul:	I'll be asking everything.
Students:	[a lot of talking and gesturing all at once]

Mrs. Glenda:	Ok you ask the ones that you think are gonna get the most mileage.
Student:	< . . . age> [overlapping talk with Mrs. Glenda]
Mrs. Glenda:	Yes, absolutely. Now is this gonna help up here? This is not the final draft too. We can add to this every day. If you come back and say, I got it. I know . . .
Rich:	[interrupts] Why would you want to add to that? You have like more than a thousand questions? [some students laugh]
Mrs. Glenda:	I don't know Rich, maybe this is the final draft.
Student:	[interrupts] That's only like fifty [questions].
Mrs. Glenda:	But you know what happens to me? I go home, I sit down, I have a mug of tea, and suddenly my brain starts working again and [snaps fingers] Oh, I wish I'd said that.
Denise:	Take a piece of paper home with you.
Mrs. Glenda:	I do. You can ask Leslie. My home has stickies all over the place [gestures placing stickies as she speaks].

The students demonstrated their enthusiasm for asking these questions in this interaction. Many talk at once about how they are planning to ask a lot of questions. Mrs. Glenda encouraged the students to think about asking questions that they thought would "get the most mileage." She did not explain what she meant by this, nor was she asked, but another student joined her and spoke with her as she said "mileage," which marked a kind of synchrony between Mrs. Glenda and the students. However, just as we see this shared understanding emerge, Rich questioned why one would ever want to add on to this chart that already had "more than a thousand questions." Mrs. Glenda responded again (as she did in introducing the chart) by personalizing the experience – by talking about what happened to her and how she continued to build on her own thinking over time. She took this opportunity to not only model and invite the students into a way of being a questioner of others but also to consider becoming a reviser of one's own thinking over time. In this last excerpt from the Questions Chart discussion, it's clear that there is one question that remained a concern for the students.

Qing:	If the reporter can't answer the questions are you gonna help the reporter?
Mrs. Glenda:	Am I gonna help the reporter? No, you guys are gonna help the reporter. [some students laugh]
Dai:	Two reporter. [i.e., there are always two reporters]
Mrs. Glenda:	No, you mean, oh yeah let's see if I'm getting this right.
Denise:	You don't need help with questions anymore.
Mrs. Glenda:	Yeah, you don't need help with questions anymore, we've got a ton of questions, but if like the reporter is really...
Denise:	Stuck.
Mrs. Glenda:	They can't construct a theory even if you guys ask them the questions, yes I will help.

Qing was still concerned about the reporters getting help if they needed it. Mrs. Glenda emphasized that although the audience members would be responsible for helping the reporters by asking questions, she would always be available for support in the event that, in Denise's words, they got "stuck." This question implies concerns about the potential limits of students' current thinking and concerns about saving face when you had no viable answers to others' questions. Would student reporters be left to flounder in the face of questions from students in the audience? With reassurance from Mrs. Glenda that she would always be there to help, the class negotiated a plan for the rest of the period and began their small-group work time together.

Day 5: Reporting. " I have lots of questions. Questions, questions, questions." The students enthusiastically embraced questioning during reporting time after their whole-class conversation about the Questions Chart. Olivia and Rosie reported for their group about the straw balance investigation that students completed using drinking straws and paper clips (see Investigation #6, p. 37).

Olivia:	Are you guys gonna see our summarizing results?
Mrs. Glenda:	Wait a sec we have a visual summary over here and that's ...
Rosie:	[interrupts] He's asking me a question.
Mrs. Glenda:	Ok, but hold on.
Qing:	**I have lots of questions.**
Student:	**Questions, questions, questions.**
Mrs. Glenda:	Ok well.
Qing:	Well do you think it's different if you put it closer or ...
Raul:	Farther?
Qing:	Yeah.
Olivia:	Close you see it will go down.

The students were so excited about asking questions that Olivia and Mrs. Glenda had a hard time focusing their attention on the visual summary the group created. Qing and Raul spoke together to pose a question, marking a co-construction practice that began to occur more and more after Day 5 (Ochs, Schieffelin, & Platt, 1979). Later during another report on Day 5, Raul blurted out as Mrs. Glenda was assigning roles, **"I've got a question already and we haven't even started yet."** As is evident in this analysis, the first five days of instruction were crucial for the students to become confident and enthusiastic questioners. After Day 5, students developed more fluidity in asking questions of one another.

Day 7: "If you talked less in the beginning, we'd have more time to talk at the end." An unusual request from the students. As time went on and questioning practices were more commonly shared among classroom members, the students asked Mrs. Glenda to spend less time talking at the beginning of a lesson so they could spend more time on their reports at the end of each session. In the following interaction on Day 7, Denise initiated and negotiated a request for herself and for her peers. Earlier that day, Denise and other students expressed frustration because they did not have enough time to report about their activities. They were running out of time every day and they were feeling increasingly frustrated about it. The following segment began when Mrs. Glenda stopped reporting time and stepped in. She was concerned because the bell just rang and not all groups had enough time to finish reporting. She brought up Denise's suggestion to the class.

Mrs. Glenda:	Ok, all right, listen we're not even close [kids keep on talking], excuse me, excuse me I'm exercising my big person rights here.
Tammy:	People are talking and...
Mrs. Glenda:	Excuse me.
Carson:	Other groups hafta go up.
Mrs. Glenda:	No way! no way! [Students want one group to stop and another to start reporting] this is like not working out and I hafta say this in response to Denise, Denise has voiced a criticism to me and I am gonna honor her criticism, can you move over just a little so I can look at her when I say this. She said that if I spent less time talking in the beginning we'd have more time talking in the end.
Denise:	We come in and just do our projects.
Mrs. Glenda:	You come in and just do your project, well I'll tell you what, how about if we come in and just get the next two groups, is that alright?
Student:	Yeah.
Student:	Yeah.
Mrs. Glenda:	Is that ok if we just do reports instead of me talking at all?
Student:	Yeah.
Carson:	Yeah that's good.
Mrs. Glenda:	That's better, so next time we'll just do reports?

Carson:	Yeah cuz cuz we every single time there's always like . . .
Steve:	There's always a group or two left over.
Mrs. Glenda:	Yeah we just don't have enough time, ok why don't you line up now and Denise, I know this has been a rough day all around the school. I don't know why.

Mrs. Glenda took time, even in this rushed moment when the class period was ending and groups had not finished reporting, to stop and "honor" Denise's criticism and the class's shared frustration. But first she had to invoke her "big person rights" to get the students to stop talking. She proposed a new beginning to the next session, allowing the students to get right to work themselves. Mrs. Glenda took the time to ask students to move so that she could look at Denise directly when she spoke. Denise reiterated Mrs. Glenda's proposal as a form of agreement and other students quickly chimed in, including Carson who had struggled with reporting so much in the early days. They all wanted more time to report and discuss their ideas together.

This was an exceptional request. The students revealed their dissatisfaction because they wanted *more* time to work together and to ask questions of one another. At the beginning of the segment above, they do not want to stop even though the bell rang. Carson suggested that they just send one more group up to the front to report. This demonstrated the value the students had come to place on their shared work and the importance of questioning each other about it. They all wanted their airtime. This marked a significant accomplishment for the class. They had become a group of students who worked together to investigate, share, and evaluate scientific explanations. They did this by adopting new ways of thinking and doing in science and new ways of being students of science.

The Creation of a Community of Questioners

The students and Mrs. Glenda started out as a collection of people in a familiar school context but an unfamiliar classroom setting. The background assumption that the teacher was responsible for asking reporters questions was challenged and explicitly replaced by new values and roles giving all community members the right and responsibility to ask reporters questions. On the surface, it seemed like a simple idea. It was assumed that students knew how to ask questions because they did it all the time outside of the classroom. But to do this in the context of the classroom was a significant departure from the typical rules of engagement in school. To complicate matters, students were to ask questions about new ways of knowing and doing that they were also in the process of making their own. The detailed moment-to-moment examination of what unfolded as students questioned other students in the classroom demonstrated the daily challenges the students and Mrs. Glenda faced as they worked together to create a community that was different from typical school science classrooms. Students did not just begin the process of asking reporters questions spontaneously, they needed help and support from Mrs. Glenda and from each other.

Mrs. Glenda introduced some new ways of knowing, doing, and being together as questioners. She valued and expected all students to participate. She assessed which students had the most difficulty and helped them find their voices in the classroom. She created an emotional climate of respect and trust within the classroom and consistently conveyed her confidence in the students. She drew on the students' ways of thinking and talking to build a web of meaning that could be shared within the classroom. The class went through a fast-paced process of getting to know one another. Over the course of the first eight days of the study, the audience members emerged as people who asked questions of reporters. To learn to do this required coordinating new intellectual practices of predicting, theorizing, summarizing results, and relating results back to original predictions and theories with new ways of conducting themselves together as a classroom, and new ways of valuing other students' ideas as well as their own. Audience members shifted from trying to offer up their own explanations and ideas about what the reporters said to actively trying to understand reporters' ideas and ask questions to clarify when they did not understand. They created a foundation of shared meaning and an emotional climate of respect, which included new intellectual concepts and practices as well as social roles and responsibilities.

Table 2. *Distribution of turns/report for students across the study.*

Days	Average Percentage of Student Turns	Range of Student Turns
2, 3, 4	61.7%	58.3–67.0%
5, 6, 7	70.3%	62.2–74.7%
8, 9, 10, 11	76.4%	69.4–87.3%

This culminated on Day 7 with a request for Mrs. Glenda to spend less time on her role of orienting students to activities so that they could spend more time talking about their ideas during reporting. Even students like Carson, who initially struggled to feel confident asking questions, wanted more time for students to discuss their ideas together. Questioning was not simply a matter of developing knowledge and skill. It was a matter of personal and social values, developing confidence, and establishing trust and respect that had to be constructed along with new knowledge and skills.

Another way of looking at how things shifted in terms of students' taking on new ways of knowing, doing, and being together is to look at the distribution of turns/report for the students across the study. Table 2 shows that over time the students' percentage of talk as measured in turns/report increased. This graphically presents how the community shifted with respect to students' role in asking each other questions about their ideas.

As Mrs. Glenda and the students developed these new ways of being, knowing, and doing together within the classroom, it had a ripple effect. This new role of students as questioners in the classroom shifted a number of other issues as well. In Chapter 3, we follow on from this central analysis of how the students became a community of questioners to investigate how this new practice surfaced other important issues as well.

3   How Ways of Knowing, Doing, and Being Emerged in the Classroom

Interpersonal Interactions and the Creation of Community, Part II

As students took up questioning each other about their ideas during reporting, we found other ways of being, doing, and knowing were opened up for renegotiation and redefinition inside the classroom. The students' interactions raised a host of issues that are taken for granted in the context of more traditional classrooms. For instance, speaking rights in a traditional classroom are well understood by fourth graders. If you raise your hand and the teacher calls on you, you have a chance to speak, most often in response to a question posed by the teacher. In our classroom context with students creating and responding to questions and Mrs. Glenda standing to the side to facilitate this process, traditional patterns of classroom speaking were no longer possible to engage. This was especially true once students developed a strong desire to ask questions and learned how to create or appropriate content critical questions. When preparing a report, students had to decide who would present each part of the report. Students had to negotiate which audience members would ask a question first when multiple hands were raised. Reporters had to determine which reporting partner would respond to the questions from the audience. These interesting dilemmas of who had the right to speak and when opened another window into better understanding how ways of knowing, doing, and being emerged together and influenced the values and rules of engagement that came to distinguish this classroom.

As we discuss the ways of knowing, doing, and being that were renegotiated as a result of the students taking up questioning, it may be tempting to view examples as highlighting either (1) knowing and doing or (2) being and doing. We understand this temptation but want to reiterate our argument that these dimensions are always being negotiated together. There is never a time when being, knowing, and doing are not in play at once. Some of the examples may spotlight one aspect more than the others but our claim is that to isolate one from the others will not provide a complete picture of learning in the classroom. To identify only those episodes where knowing and doing are highlighted or being and doing are evident would again bring us back to a fragmented and partial view. We are purposely looking at learning as being, knowing, and doing together and working to understand, in our case, how developing new ways of knowing and doing brought about new ways of being.

This chapter explores five issues that emerged as a result of students' adopting the role of questioning each other's ideas. We will focus on: (1) Negotiating and establishing speaking rights, (2) Persisting in the face of difficulty to understand and articulate ideas, (3) Taking perspectives to support the exchange and understanding of ideas, (4) Challenging ideas, and (5) Being wrong (and/or changing one's mind). We will offer examples that highlight how these new ways of being, knowing, and doing emerged across the study. Haroutunian-Gordon and Waks (in press) and their colleagues who contributed to the Special Issue on Listening for Teachers College Record discuss how teachers are challenged to take up all five of these areas. In our case, we focus on how listening for understanding and asking questions to clarify understanding framed the shared work of Mrs. Glenda and the students in our focal classroom.

Negotiating and Establishing Speaking Rights

The idea that children are important interlocutors in any setting varies by culture and historical time period. The old proverb that "children should be seen and not heard" was once a widely shared belief in the United States and recitation was a common discourse pattern in schools. Teachers would lecture or recite and students would repeat the teacher's words or respond to questions posed by the teacher (Cubberley, 1919). Progressive educational reformers, such as John Dewey (1916), questioned the use of recitation as an effective means of education. He believed that the purpose of education was to introduce and guide students through essential experiences of life in a democracy, experiences that called for active student participation and discussion. However, even today, the idea that young students have their own ideas and can and should participate in classroom discussions about these ideas is not always a widely held belief.

Research on classroom instructional patterns from the 1960s through the 1980s suggested that even during this era teachers talked for much of the time during classes (Cazden, 1988; Flanders, 1970). The most common form of interaction was the Initiation-Response-Evaluation (IRE) sequence (Mehan, 1979; Sinclair & Coulthard, 1975). Teachers initiated questions, students responded, and teachers evaluated student responses. This pattern, although characteristic of school-based interaction, would be unusual in many other contexts. It is rare, and could be perceived as bizarre and insulting, to ask questions when one already knows the answer. Therefore, the most common pattern of interaction in schools does not have an analogue outside of school settings (Lave & Wenger, 1991; Rogoff, 1990). Recent work in science and mathematics learning emphasizes the important role that discussion plays in learning (Chapin, O'Connor, & Anderson, 2009; Lemke, 1990; O'Connor & Michaels, 1993; Michaels, Shouse, & Schweingruber, 2008). Although research suggests that this is essential, it is still not necessarily a feature of regular classroom experience for most students.

This historical background helps to shape the enormous significance of the explicit negotiation of student speaking rights in the classroom we discuss here. What we saw students do and say and how we saw students come into their own as speakers in this school context was not necessarily typical of science classrooms. There were many examples of negotiating who had the right to speak at a particular time. In this section, we present the range of ways this unfolded in the classroom. At first students were trying to understand what it meant to take on their roles of question posers and responders (as we described in Chapter 2). In this chapter we address the squabbles that erupted about who had the right to speak once the students understood and felt confident as active questioners in class. Mrs. Glenda was instrumental in negotiating speaking and turn-taking throughout the time the students worked together. She positioned herself and others in ways that encouraged quiet or unsure students to find their voice. She also helped students who wanted to speak for others learn how to leave space open in a discussion for everyone. Mrs. Glenda supported audience members to question reporters if needed and she helped mediate disputes between reporting partners who both wanted to speak about the same issues for their reports.

Day 3. "I could help Carson." The first example comes from a more extended interaction we presented in Chapter 2. This was one of the earliest moments where Mrs. Glenda asserted basic values about who could participate when. Carson was having trouble understanding how to begin his report. Denise offered to help.

Denise:	***I could help Carson.***
Mrs. Glenda:	Ok ok but Denise but it's not your job to help for this thing, prediction and theory people this is your job now let's see if you can get a prediction from Carson and a theory, go ahead.

Here we see that a common practice of offering to help a fellow group member in need was not taken up. Instead, Mrs. Glenda positioned audience members as central players in successful reporting. This may seem like a relatively small move, but it had powerful consequences. First, it positioned Carson as capable on his own to deliver his report without assistance from other group members. Mrs. Glenda was concerned about Carson and believed he needed opportunities to build confidence. She set up clear distinctions of worth that valued him and his ideas and she directed the emotional support in the class to be sure he succeeded in presenting his report. Second, it elevated the idea of dialogue across groups to a central place in the classroom. This set the expectations for the rest of the discussions during the study, but by no means did it protect students from having to negotiate speaking rights in the flurry of enthusiastic debate and dialogue.

Day 5. "We're just having major technical difficulties right here. We're negotiating who owns what part of this report." As the students became more interested in their group's ideas and felt more ownership over particular processes that helped the group move their thinking further, we noticed that reporters had a hard time negotiating which person would be responsible for the most exciting parts of the report. On this day, Dai and Denise were assigned to report for their group. They had been working on a balance scale problem and made significant revisions to their theory as a result of their investigations. The investigation involved students placing one 10-gram weight on peg 6 on the left arm of the balance and two 10-gram weights on peg 3 on the right arm of the balance (see Investigation #5, p. 36). Before releasing the fulcrum, students using a weight theory predicted that the right arm would go down whereas students with a distance theory predicted that the left arm would go down. None of the students predicted that the scale would balance and, when it did, they were puzzled and amused. This unexpected finding was incredibly generative for the group as they tried to figure out how all of their predictions could have been wrong. As they began to work together, they noticed that there was a way to coordinate both weight and distance within their theory. Their new theory was "you can double the distance on one side to double the weight on the other to get the scale to balance." Dai and Denise both wanted to share this exciting news with the whole class. Their small-group investigation elevated their interest in revising their thinking and then reporting about it. They both wanted to tell the story of how their initial "wrong predictions" helped them to create their new theory. Denise was the student who first proposed this new theory, so she was very interested in reporting about the third step of relating predictions, theories, and results. Dai also wanted to report this part as it was viewed as the most exciting and new. Mrs. Glenda helped the students negotiate turn taking as they came to the front of the room, still at a stalemate.

Mrs. Glenda: [Mrs. Glenda negotiates with Dai and Denise because they are having trouble deciding who should report about each step.] *We're just having major technical difficulties right here. We're just negotiating who owns what part of this report* and um and we gotta do it because we want to get

	this done before lunch, sometimes it's really hard to compromise.
Qing:	I had that problem too but Raul and but Steven didn't care about any of the report so I just pick one.
Mrs. Glenda:	You just picked one. Ok.
Raul:	I report too.
Mrs. Glenda:	[directs this question to Dai.] Are you gonna be destroyed if you don't get to do that [the third step]?
Dai:	Yeah.
Mrs. Glenda:	Ok. [laughs a little] Ok. How about [inaudible]?
Dai:	No.
Mrs. Glenda:	I'll make it up to you, I really will, you can come down and scrounge some of my stuff down there [in my office].
Dai:	Ok. Now what do I do now? Nothing?
Mrs. Glenda:	No, no way. You do one and two.
Dai:	Where do we start? Down down here.
Mrs. Glenda:	I'll help you. Go ahead.

Using the diminutive "just" to modify her statement, Mrs. Glenda announced that students were "having major technical difficulties." By choosing these terms, Mrs. Glenda indicated to Dai and Denise and the audience that these issues are to be expected and could be overcome. Ultimately Mrs. Glenda negotiated with Dai that he could do the first two steps and come down to her office later and "scrounge some of [her] stuff" to take home with him. This demonstrated how connected the students began to feel to presenting new ideas that moved thinking further. It was increasingly difficult to decide who would present. Students wanted the chance to speak about their group's ideas to the rest of the class, especially when they were viewed as new and interesting.

Day 7. "Ok, Christie has her thing that she did, she can do it." On Day 7, Mrs. Glenda took what might seem like a radically different stance on who got to participate when. In this case, she allowed a student who was not assigned a particular role to assume it. On this day, Dai was a reporter for his group. The other student reporter was absent. Mrs. Glenda watched Christie during small-group work time build a soda straw balance and decided to invite Christie to report together with Dai. Christie had expressed to both Mrs. Glenda and Leslie that she did not like to report. However, given her successful small-group work time, Mrs. Glenda decided to position Christie as a capable and successful reporter.

Dai:	We had to build a straw balance so and we had to make it balance, and um I didn't make it balance because um there's not enough time for me to make it so um...
Mrs. Glenda:	[whispers] So do you want Christie to talk?
Dai:	But I don't know what Christie did.[1]
Mrs. Glenda:	**Ok, Christie has her thing that she did, she can do it,** go ahead.
Christie:	[reads from her notebook] My prediction was that I thought that it would not balance because when I first when I first had the straws they were not even.
Mrs. Glenda:	[whispers] Ok then you've got [inaudible].
Christie:	[again continues reading from her notebook] Because the difference distance the weight was from the end was different, I was right and it did not balance the farther out side went down [pause] they have questions for us.
Mrs. Glenda:	Ok good.
Dai:	I'll pick them, oh Raul.
Student:	Raul.
Qing:	[jumps in first before Raul] How how how many paper clips did you put on the right and the left side?

[1] The students built two soda straw balances in pairs during their small-group work time.

Christie:	I put four on each side but once the one that had uh the bigger side went down more. Yeah, Raul.
Raul:	[as Raul is asking his question there is an intercom interruption] Did your [interrupts himself] what was your theory? What was your theory?
Mrs. Glenda:	Ok, excuse me Raul was talking.
Raul:	What's your theory?
Student:	Yeah what is your theory?
Christie:	[reads from her notebook] Because of the distance the weight was from the end, from the end was different.
Raul:	Wait a minute, that's not your theory, you're telling me you're telling me the problem.
Mrs. Glenda:	Wait, I'm gonna intervene in here um Christie was talking about the straws that she was using, there was equal distance, um the straw itself and she made it balance, she did it like the scale so she had equal sides and she also had equal weights, but she had unequal places on, the paper clips were unequally placed, so it's one of those three and five kind of things, ok so . . .
Raul:	So their theory is placement, well did your findings prove your theory correct?
Mrs. Glenda:	[directed to Christie] Do you think so? Did what you think was gonna happen happen? Don't even look at that [her notebook], did what you think was gonna happen actually happen?
Christie:	Yeah [shakes her head yes].

In this interaction, Mrs. Glenda positioned Christie to take up a way of being, knowing, and doing that she was hesitant to assume. Mrs. Glenda's moves made it clear that she was determined that this was going to be a successful experience for Christie. In announcing Christie's role of reporter, she said, "Christie has her thing that she did, she can do it." This placed Christie in a position of ability and authority. Christie proceeded to make a report for her team and to respond to questions from audience members. As Raul was questioning her, Mrs. Glenda was poised to jump in and intervene to ensure that it continued to be a positive experience for Christie. Mrs. Glenda was targeting opportunities to allow Christie to re-evaluate her capabilities, develop confidence, and embrace her voice within the community. She did this by conferring speaking rights at a time when Christie would have otherwise remained silent.

Day 9: "Don't cut in on me, I'm first." Olivia and Rosie were presenting on their group's work to build a strong but flexible soda straw bridge (see Investigation #8, p. 38). The conversation had been going on for some time when audience members Raul and Qing both made bids to speak.

Mrs. Glenda:	And I should be hearing questions about results and I should hear about comparing results to predictions.
Raul:	Well, I have something to say.
Student:	Ok.
Raul:	I've got something to say.
Rosie:	Qing.
Raul:	Well you see . . .
Qing:	**Don't cut in on me, I'm first.**
Raul:	I don't care.

As students began to get comfortable asking questions and sharing ideas, there were more instances where students had to negotiate who had a turn to speak. Raul and Qing were in the same small group and therefore spent a lot of time working together. They had developed a rapport with one another. This episode, although direct in communicating a disagreement about whose turn it was to speak, was not malicious or even particularly tense. Both Qing and Raul enjoyed discussing ideas with other classmates and were vocal participants in the classroom. In this case, neither student wanted to yield the floor to give the other a chance to talk. Although the reporters had called on Qing, Raul continued to share his idea. The opposite happened in the last example, when Qing asked a question when Raul had been called on by the reporter. Mrs. Glenda was talking to another student and either did not hear the interchange between Raul and Qing or decided not to intervene. Both Raul and Qing were consistent, confident questioners in the classroom and Mrs. Glenda may have decided to allow them to work it out together.

Raul:	Well you see when you're putting all the weight it's makin' it go down but what if you tried it on the sides, you know?
Qing:	You mean like it.
Raul:	Like when you're putting all the weight, if the weight's pushing down but what if you like put more on this side then it would lean like that you see?
Steven:	Raul you keep cuttin' in front of Qing.
Raul:	Like.
Qing:	[inaudible]
Steven:	Raul, Qing's tryin' to say somethin.
Qing:	[inaudible] [Qing places something on the bridge] ta da [Materials hit the floor.]
Raul:	You see the bridge isn't stable that way, it tips like that.
Tammy:	Stop you're makin' it.
Steven:	Raul [inaudible].
Raul:	If a car drove on this side of the bridge it would fall, see? [Many children begin to talk at once. It is difficult to distinguish their voices.]
Student:	If there was a [inaudible].
Student:	But if it were a real bridge it wouldn't fall.
Qing:	Do you think it would?
Steven:	If it's flexible it won't.
Student:	It's not a real bridge.
Qing:	Do you think it would?
Olivia:	If we were outside and we saw a real bridge.
Rosie:	It wouldn't fall.

Olivia:	It wouldn't fall cause it has the right.
Raul:	It could fall.
Steven:	What happens if it's not flexible?
Raul:	It could fall.
Rosie:	One at a time please.
Raul:	People can make mistakes they can make it fall.
Steven:	I know if it's not flexible it can fall
Dai:	It's balanced, it's not balanced.
Steven:	If it's not flexible it can fall.
Rosie:	Yeah that's right but um…
Qing:	Meeeeeeeee [raising her hand].
Rosie:	You're raising your hand and we tell you, Qing Qing.
Qing:	Do you think if you, do you think if you put like that over here and one over here that it's more strong?

In this back and forth interaction between the reporters, other audience members, and Qing and Raul, we see Raul consistently stepping forward to express his ideas. However, Qing joined him to ask questions. Qing worked together with Raul to explore his ideas whereas Steven kept trying to tell Raul that he was cutting Qing off. It's not clear if she felt that way at this point. Many students had things they wanted to say and they were jockeying for a position to get space on the floor to share their thinking and proposals with the others. At the end of this excerpt, Qing raised her hand and said "meeeeeee" in a very pronounced way – getting Rosie's attention and a clear invitation to ask her own question. Rosie called on Qing and indicated that they had already told her to ask her question ("you're raising your hand and we tell you, Qing Qing"). Here we see that these new ways of knowing, being, and doing brought on new challenges – how to negotiate airtime so that all students who wanted to speak had an opportunity to do so.

Day 10: "What were you gonna say, Rosie?" This episode, used in the introduction to the book, showed that although students had disagreements about whose turn it was to present, they also began to offer one another opportunities to speak up at key points in time. In this episode, Denise was checking predictions and theories. She positioned Rosie as an important theorist who had a different point of view from her reporting partner, Rich.

Denise:	Rosie was gonna say one and then Rich was gonna say one. Rosie what was your theory?
Rich:	We already said it, I said it.
Denise:	They were both gonna say a theory.
Mrs. Glenda:	Do you think they had the same theory or different theories?
Denise:	Different.
Mrs. Glenda:	Excuse me, time out there's an excellent point being made here, Denise thinks that there's two theories over here.
Denise:	Because you were gonna say one and Raul was gonna say one.
Rich:	My name's . . .
Student:	Rich.
Rich:	Not Raul.
Student:	Rich.
Rich:	I already said it.
Denise:	***What were you gonna say Rosie?*** What were you gonna say?
Rich:	Everybody knows what I said right?
Student:	No.
Student:	Shhh.
Student:	Not me not me.
Rosie:	Well, I don't know which one because . . .
Denise:	Why did you think that was gonna happen?
Rich:	Because we didn't even start yet when we predicted.
Denise:	You made your theory I want to hear Rosie's.

Here Denise engaged in a powerful way of being, knowing, and doing by accepting her role as questioner and positioning Rosie as a competent and important thinker whose theory was necessary to fully investigate, understanding, and evaluate the merits of different scientific explanations. Denise functioned in what might be considered a teacher's role, positioning Rosie competently to take on important and necessary intellectual work in science.

Over the course of the study, the students joined Mrs. Glenda in negotiating and establishing speaking rights and in offering each other an important voice in the construction of the community and the space of intellectual ideas to be explored. IRE (Mehan, 1979) exchanges were rare. Instead, the students and Mrs. Glenda engaged in dialogues that often required them to explicitly decide who had the right to speak and when. This was essential social, intellectual, and emotional work that prepared students to develop knowledge, skills, and the willingness to put themselves out there in an effort to discuss and debate their scientific ideas.

Persisting in the Face of Difficulty to Understand and Articulate Ideas

Another change that students' questioning other students initiated was student effort to fully understand each other's ideas. "I'm confused," "I don't get what she said," and "I'm satisfied" were comments we heard regularly in this classroom, but not necessarily at first. These are uncommon student speaking patterns in traditional classroom discourse (Cazden, 1988). As students began the process of asking others questions, as we discussed in Chapter 2, they also had to monitor their own understanding of others' ideas. They had to shift from speaking about their own thoughts to actively seeking to understand and articulate the thoughts of others. If they did not understand what other students said and meant, they could not possibly ask relevant and interesting questions. At times this was a messy and uncomfortable process, leading to feelings of frustration when confusion and misunderstanding reigned. At other times, there were breakthroughs and exclamations of "I'm satisfied" and "I get it" that punctuated the room. These comments were the linguistic markers of students' developing persistence, patience, and pronouncements of progress as they worked toward the joint goal of sharing understanding. This way of being a person included significant metacognitive work to monitor one's own understanding of other's ideas. It was modeled and supported by Mrs. Glenda at first, and over time, became the primary work of the students themselves. The following examples draw from the latter half of the study to highlight how students' emerged as people who were determined to understand each other's ideas within this classroom context.

Day 5: "I don't get your, what are you doing?" By Day 5, the students were well on their way to feeling more comfortable with the idea of asking reporters questions. Before this report occurred, earlier that day, the students had created the questions chart to help them record what kinds of questions they could ask in each of their roles (see Chapter 2, p. 98). But, with each step toward more fully embracing their role as questioners, the students began to realize the need to pinpoint their own confusion and ask questions to clarify their understanding of students' ideas and intentions during reporting. In the following example, Rosie and Olivia were reporting for their group about a soda straw balance (see Investigation #6, p. 37) that they made together with group members Rich and Tammy. The students in the audience were confused about what the activity involved because this was the first day of the second set of activities and they were the first group to report about this activity. Rosie presented an initial report. Olivia asked a question of the audience.

Rosie:	Ok, today we had to build a straw balance, a straw with a pin, we push it through it, through the straw, Rich did it, I thought that at first the pins would balance, and our results was that it balanced.
Olivia:	Do you think it will balance?
Raul:	I mean your your your ...
Olivia:	Do you think this one will balance?
Raul:	No, well ...
Rich:	Just say that the straws were the same size.
Olivia:	The straws are even.
Raul:	Yeah, ok.

Olivia:	Do you think it'll balance?
Raul:	Yeah, yeah.
Student:	No.
Olivia:	It did balance.
Student:	Yes I got it right.
Qing:	*I don't really understand what you were asking.*
Steven:	*I know.*
Denise:	*I don't get your report either.*
Qing:	*I don't get your, what are you doing?*
Olivia:	Today our activity was um balancing with the paper clips,
Rosie:	See [Rosie holds up the task card so that the other students can see it].
Olivia:	We had to um build a straw balance, we had to use a straw and put a pin through it and...
Rosie:	Hang a paper clip hang a paper clip on one end of the straw.
Olivia:	With um these two blocks [students are putting up a demonstration] Like this [pause] Rosie give me another one [pause] yeah yeah that Rosie.
Olivia:	Rosie get me another one.
Rich:	Another what, paper clip?
Steven:	What was your theory?
Olivia:	No, another block.
Mrs. Glenda:	Can somebody repeat for me the question that was asked cuz I didn't hear it very well.
Olivia:	She didn't understand what
Steven:	What the activity is.
Olivia:	And so we were, I told her what it was.

Rosie and Olivia charged headlong into their report, describing the activity to the students in the audience. As they reported, they also began to ask the students in the audience questions about what the audience expected to happen to the straws when they were attached together with the pin at the center of each straw. Raul was able to join in with the reporters. However, Qing, Denise, and Steven were all uncertain about the reporters' question and perhaps even about their general approach to reporting ("I don't get your report either."). Generally, the audience members did not understand what the reporters were doing. Rosie and Olivia then began the process of reorienting the audience to the activity by describing it again in words, holding up the activity card they had used, and also creating a demonstration in front of the class. Mrs. Glenda was not involved at all in this reorientation. The audience members did all the work of expressing their confusion and then the reporters repaired the confusion by carefully explaining and demonstrating for the audience. At the end of the interaction, Mrs. Glenda asked the students to repeat the question they had been discussing. Olivia and Steven easily presented the question to Mrs. Glenda.

Steven's question about the group's theory was picked up next as the students asked the reporters about their intellectual work now that they understood the activity.

Raul:	I didn't hear a theory.
Steven:	I just said I just said what's your theory?
Mrs. Glenda:	What was the theory, ok, what was the theory?
Qing:	I heard it.
Mrs. Glenda:	You heard it?
Qing:	Yeah.
Mrs. Glenda:	You wanna try repeating it?
Student:	You heard a theory?
Qing:	I thought I heard in [she points to Rosie], I thought it will balance, that's what I heard, is that right? [Rosie nods yes]
Qing:	Haaaaa. [Qing claps her hands. Rosie is smiling at her.]
Student:	Prediction.
Raul:	That's the prediction.
Mrs. Glenda:	Ok, you thought...

Raul:	That's the prediction, that's not the theory.
Denise:	Why they thought it would balance.
Raul:	Yeah, why they think it will balance.
Steven:	That's the prediction. [A number of students start talking at once all agreeing that this is the prediction, not the theory.]
Olivia:	And I thought that it would we thought it would balance because I mean...
Steven:	We want your theory.
Olivia:	Because it was right in the center because see like right now it's staying like that alone and [inaudible].
Mrs. Glenda:	It's still not clear to you yet.
Raul:	Well, you're saying, well you're saying that your theory is that if if they're even on the same if they're even on each side then it will balance.
Mrs. Glenda:	Is that your theory? Equal distance apart?
Olivia:	Yeah, our theory is that equal dis dis dis ditnance [Olivia stutters on distance. During the whole questioning session between Raul and Olivia, Steven and Denise are carrying on their own conversation on task regarding predicting and theorizing.]
Raul:	Distance.
Mrs. Glenda:	Distance.
Olivia:	Of the parts will make it balance.
Mrs. Glenda:	Yeah, that's her theory. Is that...
Raul:	*Ok, I'm satisfied.*
Mrs. Glenda:	Ok.

Raul, Denise, and Steven all recognized that what the reporters were calling their theory was actually what the class understood to be a prediction. These students persisted with their line of questioning and provided support, together with Mrs. Glenda, so that reporters could articulate why they thought the soda straw scale would balance. Raul played a central role in this, revoicing (O'Connor & Michaels, 1996) or repeating Olivia's theory statement to check his own understanding of what she meant. After checking his understanding, Raul stated, "ok, I'm satisfied," clearly marking that he understood and that Olivia had provided something that would count as a theory in their classroom context. This way of being, knowing, and doing built on Mrs. Glenda's invitation to the audience to view their roles as similar to hers. The students began to signal this by explicitly marking satisfaction of their understanding of another group's ideas.

Day 7: "What does she mean?" Although some students easily moved into the roles of asking and answering questions from other students, others had a more difficult time. The following interaction between Mrs. Glenda and Christie demonstrated how students in the reporting role looked to Mrs. Glenda for support when they could not understand what audience members were asking.

Tammy:	How did you know it [the prediction] was correct?
Olivia:	How did you know it was correct?
Christie:	*What does she mean?* [looking to Mrs. Glenda]
Mrs. Glenda:	She means, she means how did you know
Olivia:	How did you know, how did you know this was all of you
Dai:	Correct, how did you know you did it right?
Mrs. Glenda:	Wait a sec, it's great to ask questions but let the poor girl answer.
Christie:	Because I guessed it would go down and it did.

Here Mrs. Glenda and the students worked together to ensure that Christie understood the question. In this case, the clarification was started by Mrs. Glenda but finalized by Olivia and Dai in a way that distributed the question across utterances and speakers (Ochs, Schieffelin, & Platt, 1979). It was interesting that although Christie turned to Mrs. Glenda for help, that by Day 7 many of the students automatically jumped in with their support as well. The fact that the students co-construct this question demonstrates a developing level of shared understanding and synchrony in the classroom. Mrs. Glenda marked this enthusiasm with a caution to give Christie a chance to answer.

Day 9: "Your theory is why why." During Day 9, Raul articulated his theory about their tipi activity (see Investigation #10, p. 39) with Steven's help.

Raul:	My theory was that it was gonna that it was gonna fall, that it wasn't gonna stay up.
Steven:	That was your prediction.
Raul:	My prediction.
Steven:	**Your theory is why why**.
Raul:	My ok, my prediction was that it was gonna fall over because in the middle what's holdin' it up is putty and um the and the um the string, we had ta put string across the straw which was in putty which was holding up the straw, and the string was pulling it like strong and stuff, but the um it was pulling it too strong and like the putty wasn't holding it enough and the straw would start to bend in one direction, and so that's the main structure of the house, that's what's holding everything up so if that fell then the house would fall with it, so I thought it was going to fall.
Mrs. Glenda:	That's an amazing theory.
Olivia:	That is a theory?
Mrs. Glenda:	It's a heck of a theory, honey, it's a heck of theory.
Raul:	It's a theory and prediction.
Steven:	It's kinda both.

Earlier we presented an example of Raul reminding others about the distinction between predictions and theories. Here, it was Raul who needed that kind of support from Steven. As students began to coordinate new terms and concepts, they helped remind one another about meanings and supported one another to be clear in using them. Here Raul got confused and that was okay. Steven supported Raul to articulate his ideas clearly. Mrs. Glenda glanced up at the video camera where Leslie was and smiled when Steven said to Raul, "That was your prediction. Your theory is why why." Watching students transforming participation was exciting, especially for students like Steven who often deferred to others in the classroom.

Taking Perspectives

A central way of being, knowing, and doing that assisted students in both asking and answering questions was the ability to take another's perspective. In the following examples, we see some examples of perspective-taking by the students throughout the study.

Baseline Day: "You see it depends [on] the way you're facing." In this segment, the students were trying to establish which was the left side and which was the right side of a balance scale. This is an issue because the students are gathered on the floor in a configuration that did not allow them to share the same vantage point to observe the scale. They were working on a balance scale problem with one 10-gram weight on the third peg on the right and two 10-gram weights on the third peg on the left.

Olivia:	Two grams of weight on number three on the left.
Qing:	This is the left.
Rich:	That's the right.
Raul:	[exasperated tone] **You see it depends the way you're facing**. If you're facing this way this is your left, if you're facing that way, this is your left (motions with his arms as he speaks indicating which side would be left).
Mrs. Glenda:	Excellent point. Excuse me, we can come to an agreement with that point right now because forevermore when we're doing things you hafta be in agreement about what's left and what's right.

Establishing the left and the right side of the balance scale was a point of utmost importance as the students began this series of investigations together. Raul gestured and explained that left and right was relative to one's position to the balance scale. Raul expressed his perspective with a tone of frustration, as if to say, "don't you get it!" However, by the end of this segment, Raul had shifted from facing away from the group, to using pointing to indicate left and right, to sitting up on his knees facing the group, physically demonstrating engagement in the activity. Mrs. Glenda followed up on Raul's contribution legitimizing the importance of perspective and positioning Raul's comment as an "excellent point." She suggested that it would be crucial to identify and agree on left and right from that point forward. This example engaged ways of knowing, doing, and being through Raul's physical, intellectual, and emotional reorientation to the rest of his classmates.

Day 5: "*Qing just said if you put it on two chairs to see if it will make a difference and that's what I was tryin' to do.*" Olivia and Rosie were reporting for their group about a soda straw balance they had constructed (see Investigation #6, p. 37). The group had problems reconstructing their apparatus for the class because once they constructed it and placed the stationary straw on blocks, they realized that the larger size paper clips they were using in the small-group work were too big for the space between the blocks and the table in the demonstration. Qing suggested that the group could try placing their balance between two classroom chairs to see if that might work. The class shifts their focus away from the demonstration that was not working well and began asking questions about their work in their small group to coordinate their predictions, theories, and results. Rich was frustrated with this and wanted to get the demonstration to work using Qing's suggestion.

Mrs. Glenda:	Talk through what you're doing, please, Rich, what's ever right here [points to her head] just tell us, ok?
Rich:	Well ***Qing just said if you put it on two chairs to see if it'll make a difference and that's what I was tryin' to do*** but the paper clips fall off.
Mrs. Glenda:	They fall off but can you I mean Olivia just told me that what you thought was gonna happen didn't happen.

Olivia:	Because we thought it would balance and right now when we showed you right here.
Mrs. Glenda:	It won't.
Rich:	It couldn't.
Mrs. Glenda:	And so Rich is telling the group that he changed the experiment so it could balance, you need more room for the paper clips, is that what you're telling me, you need to get the wooden blocks up higher? Are you guys all satisfied with that?
Raul:	Yeah.

Rich took up other students' ideas to try them out and spontaneously test them. The students began to adopt each other's perspectives and explored each other's ideas as a way to further their own thinking and experimentation. This was not necessarily a natural or easy process, however, as the next example from Day 5 demonstrated.

Later in Day 5: "That looks pretty true." Day 5 was a pivotal day in the reporting sessions. One group put forward a theory that, for the first time, took into account both weight and distance from the fulcrum. Denise and Dai, the reporters, presented their group's theory, generated in response to what Siegler (1985) calls a "conflict balance" problem. In this case, the students were asked to work on a balance scale problem that had one 10-gram weight on peg number six on the left arm and two 10-gram weights on peg number three on the right arm of a balance scale (see Investigation #5, p. 36). Two students in Denise's group predicted that the side with the most weight would tilt down. Denise and another group member predicted that the side with the greatest distance would tilt down. Neither prediction proved correct, so the group set out to make sense of their confusing results. They revised their initial "weight" and "distance" theories by suggesting that you can "double the distance [on one side] to double the weight [on the other side.]" Denise presented her revised theory to the class. It prompted a lively discussion.

Denise:	One on six. It balanced, it balanced. I thought it was gonna go down here because of the distance but it really balanced because of this was 20 grams and now if you

see that up ta from one to three would be 10 grams and from three to six would be 20 grams and you just double the distance against the weight and it's it's equal. [Mrs. Glenda claps.]

Rich: That's not true.

Denise: Yes it is. [A disagreement breaks out here within the group with some children agreeing with the theory and others refuting it.]

Raul: ***That looks pretty true.***

Denise: Yes it is, it is.

Raul: If you put two, if you put two weights on two and then you put one weight on four on the other it would balance.

Rich argued that this wasn't true, but Raul said, "that looks pretty true." Raul took up Denise's theory and went on to suggest that it would balance if they changed the problem and put 20 grams on number two on one side of the balance scale and 10 grams on number four on the other. Mrs. Glenda suggested that they experiment with the problem Raul suggested.

Mrs. Glenda: Shall we check?

Raul: Yeah.

Dai: No it won't.

Mrs. Glenda: We shall check.

Raul: Go ahead.

Dai: No it won't.

Mrs. Glenda: Put it on table and let's check.

Student: No it won't.

Olivia: What made you know that?

Mrs. Glenda: Go ahead.

Dai: I said it won't.

Mrs. Glenda: You say it won't, let's see.

Dai: I say it won't.

Denise: I say it will.

Dai:	I say it won't.
Mrs. Glenda:	Why? Why do you think Raul, why do you know it?
Raul:	Because because they just said that and also the thum thum thum thum thum [everyone laughs, the room is buzzing with excitement].
Raul:	The place the placement like, like when I when I did the, don't pinch me [said to neighboring child].
Mrs. Glenda:	Ok.
Raul:	When I when I when I was using the scale . . .
Mrs. Glenda:	The seesaw scale or this [balance] scale?
Raul:	The seesaw scale, the placement of the um person, like I was heavier right, so I would go down, and if I moved to the middle and Steven stayed where I was, I me and him would balance because it would be like [motions with arms].
Denise:	What if Steven's not the same weight as you?
Steven:	He wasn't but we still balanced.
Raul:	We're not the same weight I'm 71 and he's . . .
Denise:	Well if he's lesser than you.
Raul:	I'm 71 and he's 62.
Steven:	. . . and we still balanced.
Dai:	You're 71?
Raul:	Yeah I'm 71.
Mrs. Glenda:	Are you making the connection, you are making the connection between what you see here and what you did in the other room [the seesaw activity]?
Denise:	I don't think he understands what I said.
Mrs. Glenda:	I think he understands real good what you said. Real good. Ok can you say can you tell us again where she should be putting these things? They did three and six, you wanna do two and four now?

Raul suggested a parallel problem to test the generalizability of Denise's group's theory. This prompted some disagreement from other students. Some students did not think it would balance whereas other students did think it would balance. Mrs. Glenda suggested that they try this test. All the while there was a palpable excitement in the room. Some students, like Olivia, were trying to ask questions and get responses from the reporters in the midst of all this activity. Students were shouting their predictions out loud and then Mrs. Glenda, picking up on Olivia's question, "what made you know that" asked Raul to explain why he thought it would balance. Raul made a link between Denise's theory and an experience that he and Steven had when they were working on the seesaw activity (see Investigation #7, p. 37). Although Raul and Steven were not the same weight, they were able to balance by positioning themselves in particular spots on the seesaw. Therefore, he thought that it would be possible to take different weights and make them balance on the scale. Testing Denise's theory of doubling weights and distances would allow them to see if unequal weights could balance in more than one way on the balance scale too.

In this interchange, the students were actively engaging a way of being that is essential to the scientific enterprise – being people who create theories through replication of findings and develop theories with broad applicability. Denise emerged as a person who engaged surprising or puzzling results to push her theorizing further. Raul emerged as a person who took up Denise's perspective in light of his own experiences and tried on her new set of ideas. All the students' ways of being, knowing, and doing fused together in a profound and distributed phronetic act. It was an act of joy, excitement, and skepticism. It is challenging to convey just how much this classroom was buzzing with this breakthrough that was at once intellectual and emotional. This complex set of inter-relationships, all happening at once, created a kind of student engagement and energy that we had not seen in the classroom before this point. Denise did not understand Raul's link to the seesaw activity, and in the midst of the excitement, Mrs. Glenda did not fully pursue this line of reasoning to help make Raul's logic available to all the other students. Raul spontaneously transferred his learning and was able to explain this to Mrs. Glenda. Even though the rest of the students did not have full access to his explanation, the idea that he offered it in this moment of intellectual and emotional energy demonstrates that transfer can and does happen. This was the first time that students began to coordinate weight and distance as factors that explained the balance. It was also the first time that students had been so animated in the process of discussing their intellectual ideas and actively demonstrated how they could put them to immediate use in the form of a test of generalizability. In closing that day, Mrs. Glenda said, "I've got goosebumps, guys, you were awesome, awesome." She was thrilled to see these new ideas produce such a lively social and intellectual debate and discussion.

Day 7: "It could balance if you would have placed it a different way." In this excerpt on Day 7, Raul listened to Rich's point of view and explained how it made sense to him. The students were discussing a balance scale problem with four 10-gram weights on the first peg on the right and two 10-gram weights on the third peg on the left (see Investigation #3, p. 36 for a similar problem that varies both weight and distance from the fulcrum). This was toward the end of a lengthy discussion where Qing had made a mistake in reporting about the problem they were using. This confused some students and made Rich continue to argue that his perspective (that the scale would balance) was accurate.

Raul:	It [the scale] could balance it could balance, it's the placement but you the way they're placed, the way they're placed it will not balance but *it could balance if you would have placed it a different way*.
Qing:	[inaudible] This kind of question, this is my theory, ok?
Raul:	He is right though, it could balance if you placed it the right way, but the way we had placed it, it wouldn't balance.
Rich:	Yeah but when you were up there you said that this was forty and that was six, fifty or somethin'.

Raul: Yeah this was supposed to be a 4 times 10 equals forty and then that's supposed to be a sixty.

Rich: Yeah so you wrote it wrong.

Raul: So it still wouldn't balance.

Raul communicated that he understood Rich's perspective and could imagine a scenario where the scale would balance if the weights were placed at distances that were different from the problem at hand. However, at the same time, he was also clear that Rich's perspective did not hold for the particular problem under consideration. Raul combined sophisticated ways of knowing, being, and doing here to produce a remarkable episode in the class. He respected, understood, and applied Rich's argument and gave it ample consideration. At the same time, he clearly explained why, in this particular problem, Rich's argument was not applicable. This episode occurred at the beginning of Day 7, the day that Rich challenged so much that Mrs. Glenda and the other students stopped him from continuing and commented explicitly on the fine line between nit-picky divisiveness and productive debate and discussion. The seeds for that episode were already evident here as Rich asserted that "yeah, so you wrote it *wrong*" trying to position himself as "right" and the reporting group, and Qing in particular, as "wrong." Raul tried to prevent this episode from happening by thoughtfully engaging Rich's argument and demonstrating how it could work in a different problem context. Because the students had already come to expect Rich as a challenger (see Chapter 4 where we discuss Rich's challenging further) who could be disagreeable, this intellectual move had an underlying social-emotional intention, to diffuse Rich's challenging behavior in a case where it could not possibly lead to a productive discussion. In this case, it did not work. Rich continued on and escalated his challenging behavior. Nevertheless, Raul's move to take Rich's perspective early in the conversation in an attempt to assuage Rich's tendency to plunge into challenging involved astute on-the-fly assessments of other student's ways of being, knowing, and doing in the classroom.

Day 9: "She's saying that if...". On Day 9, Raul again took another student's perspective. In this case, he helped Rosie articulate her ideas and legitimized her reasoning in describing her soda straw bridge (see Investigation #8, p. 38). The rest of the class did not understand what she was trying to say. This was not an unusual experience for Rosie. Raul used his understanding of Rosie's ideas to position her as a competent thinker whose ideas have merit in the classroom.

Rosie:	Ok, if you if you um do a bridge and you do a straws, you made a big bridge do you think if you came into the news and then [inaudible] do you think it would fall?
Christie:	Yeah.
Denise:	Would you repeat that question in a shorter question?
Rosie:	Ok, if you were makin' a bridge and it takes you two days to build it, the whole day, and you make a large bridge and then you like do it like this bridge where is it.
Olivia:	It's on the thing.
Rosie:	Ok, there, that one down there [pointing to bridge].
Denise:	This one?
Rosie:	The other one.
Denise:	This one?
Rosie:	Yes, that one do you think that...
Qing:	It will be more stronger?
Rosie:	No, if the news came um if you came out in the news and then the reporters came, the real reporters [inaudible] from the news came to you and there are so many people who want to see and [Christie sneezes – inaudible] really hard, do you think it would [inaudible]?
Denise:	I can't even understand that.
Mrs. Glenda:	Do you want me to do, here let me paraphrase?
Olivia:	Oh my God that is a long question.

Mrs. Glenda:	Yeah but I know what she's saying.
Raul:	I know what she's saying too.
Mrs. Glenda:	What is she saying?
Raul:	**She's saying that if** you had a straw um a straw bridge that you hafta make it really strong because she's saying that if there a lot of reporters and stuff and if they were looking at your bridge and if they were blowing then if, she wants to know if the bridge would fall over or if it would stay up.

Raul stepped in to rearticulate the question Rosie was trying to ask the reporters. He took his lead from Mrs. Glenda who clearly was stepping in to value Rosie and her ideas after several students comment that they don't understand Rosie. In this case, Mrs. Glenda was able to turn over the work of valuing Rosie and her ideas to Raul. He used reported speech (Wertsch, 1991) to mark that he was repeating what Rosie said, "she's saying that if. . . ." Rosie was trying to set up a hypothetical situation of a bridge that was actually completed, set up, and tested. She presented a scenario where hypothetical news reporters came to see and test the bridge. Raul was able to take Rosie's point-of-view and help the rest of the class understand her question. Mrs. Glenda smiled and looked up at the video camera toward Leslie when Raul explained and rephrased Rosie's question for the audience. Raul had done the teacher's job and Mrs. Glenda seemed very pleased that this had happened so spontaneously. Raul stands out as a student who was often taking the perspective of others. This will be discussed further in Chapter 4 when we present Raul's case study.

Challenging Ideas

Through the process of asking questions of one another, the students began to see that they did not always understand other students' ideas. This led to opportunities to ask clarifying questions and to take others' perspectives to better understand and explain ideas. Asking questions and gaining understanding also brought about the chance to disagree with or challenge other's ideas. Challenging is an interesting practice. As a way of knowing, it can be crucial to the intellectual process through which the class creates new and exciting intellectual products. It provides an opportunity for skepticism and doubt, two important habits of mind in science, to be more fully explored. As Dewey (1933) writes, "one can think reflectively only when one is willing to endure suspense and to undergo the trouble of uncertainty" (p. 16). However, challenging is often socially charged, bringing to the surface latent power and authority that can be viewed as confrontational and disruptive to productive collaboration. The confluence of these contradictory forces in the classroom made it easier to see how ways of knowing and being were intimately interconnected and could work together or at cross purposes in the classroom.

Coordinating values and beliefs about challenging while providing opportunities for students to learn how to communicate their challenges in an emotional tone that supported discussion, rather than shutting it down, was essential. In many cases, this valuing happened implicitly through the activity structure and content, distribution of student roles, and Mrs. Glenda's guidance and facilitation. The implicit values created a sense that ideas may come into conflict and that these conflicts should be discussed together to support the students and Mrs. Glenda to better understand one another, as Raul did with Rich's perspective in the previous section. This implicit structuring approach was similar to Matthews' (1980, 1984) approach to discussing philosophical questions with elementary age students. Matthews began by posing a philosophical question and then engaged the students as partners in a debate that by its very nature required students to bring up as many ideas as possible, naturally with some in conflict with others. This became an expectation of the philosophical quest – people will not always agree. And, even more important, the value that it is okay to disagree became an essential feature of Matthews' work and our science classroom.

Although disagreement was expected and viewed as productive, there were times when the energy around challenging moved from a simmer to a rolling boil that threatened to unravel into a quagmire of resentment and hurt feelings. At those moments, Mrs. Glenda facilitated discussions that explicitly discussed valued ways of knowing, being, and doing with respect to challenging to ensure that

Figure 4. Three 10-gram weights on third peg to right; two 10-gram weights on fifth peg to left.

it remained a practice with great promise for building understanding in the classroom.

Rich, Raul, and Qing, challenged others (often each other) in the classroom. Rich was responsible for over 50 percent of the total number of challenges. Therefore, these students figure prominently in this discussion.

Day 4: "It's not true what you say . . . " On Day 4, Qing and Steven were reporting about a balance beam problem that had two 10-gram weights on number 5 on the left side and three 10-gram weights on number 3 on the right side (see Figure 4). After Qing and Steven finished reporting and took some questions from the audience, Rich jumped in to say for the second time, "I don't get what she said." Raul offered to tell Rich their theory even though he was not assigned the role of reporter and, up until this point, had not entered the conversation to support the reporters. Qing and Steven had explained their ideas already but Rich claimed he still did not understand. Raul's explanation prompted Rich to immediately challenge the group's theory. We pick up the conversation as Raul was explaining the group's theory to Rich.

Raul:	Two weights right here, wait two weights on the left on what side? [Qing is holding the directions while Raul is placing the weights on the scale] two ten gram weights on five, three five, and three, two on three or . . .
Qing:	Three on three.
Raul:	Three on three, you see this one.
Student:	This side's gonna go down.

Raul:	This one this one's heavier [indicating the right side] but since this one's put out here [indicating the left side] and this one's close to this one [the distance out on each side], it would make this one [left side] go down if you let it go, watch, if you let it go, this side [indicating left] goes down.
Rich:	**It's not true what you say** because…
Steven:	Yep.
Mrs. Glenda:	Say say what if.
Rich:	What if it's not true what you say? Because you could take one of them gram ten grams off of the one that's on the five and the other one would probably go down or it would be equal.
Raul:	That's because it's heavier.
Rich:	That's what you said?
Raul:	Yeah.
Rich:	You said the farther up the more the weight.
Raul:	Yeah I said the weight or the placement.

The students were at the beginning of their struggle to coordinate and communicate the complex relationship between weight and distance in explaining balance. Throughout this conversation, it was not clear if the students understood one another. Rich's challenge was an attempt to prompt for clarification and explication. He took the general theory that Raul's group put forward about distance and thought about alternatives where it may not hold. Mrs. Glenda prompted Rich to frame his challenge as a question, suggesting that he say, "what if" instead of blurting out his challenge. She was working to help Rich frame his challenge in a manner that would be less likely to make the reporters feel like they were "on the spot." She was also shaping pro-collaboration socio-scientific norms that would support students to productively engage each other's ideas (see Yackel & Cobb, 1996). The mood was one of careful thinking and attempting to question others to achieve understanding. At this point, no one was reacting defensively to the challenges that were placed on the table. They added to the ongoing discussion of difficult ideas.

Day 5: "That's not true." As discussed earlier, Day 5 was a pivotal day in the reporting sessions. Denise's group's "double the distance [on one side] to double the weight [on the other side]" theory prompted significant discussion, debate, and problem solving during reporting. As they presented their new theory to the class, Rich, acting as an audience member responsible for checking the reporter's summary of results, challenged their findings.

> *Denise:* It balanced, it balanced. I thought it was gonna go down here because of the distance but it really balanced because of, this was 20 grams and now if you see that from one to three would be 10 grams and from three to six would be 20 grams and you just double the distance against the weight and it's it's equal.
>
> *Rich:* **That's not true.**
>
> *Denise:* Yes it is.

What followed after Rich's challenge directed the conversation toward testing the theory as a class to try out this new perspective offered by Denise's group. He was not the only student to have significant doubts about Denise's group's new theory. They gathered a balance scale to test another similar problem that Raul suggested. The whole class made predictions and Raul offered his interpretation of Denise's theory before the fulcrum was released and the outcome was observed (see p. 125 for this part of the discussion). This was the beginning of the students' attempt to coordinate weight and distance in theories that accounted for the balance scale's behavior. The students reflected on what each theory could explain and set out to test their generalizability. Dewey (1933) describes reflectivity as "the kind of thinking that consists in turning a subject over in the mind and giving it serious consecutive consideration" (p. 3). Challenging was an important part of pushing for this deep intellectual work.

Day 6: "I disagree because…" On Day 6, Tammy and Rich were reporting about the seesaw activity (see Investigation #7, p. 37). Olivia and Rosie were group members who also contributed to the report. Qing was assigned the role of checking predictions and theories. Tammy was having a hard time articulating her group's theory. Qing provided support for Tammy to articulate a theory at first, but then challenged the theory that Tammy offered.

Qing:	I can explain it, well like your prediction, you already have a prediction, why you think that prediction?
Rich:	Because it was true.
Tammy:	Because of the weight.
Olivia:	The weights that we had.
Qing:	**I disagree.**
Rich:	The weight.
Qing:	**I disagree.**
Rich:	Well you don't know.
Qing:	**I disagree because** when I was when our group it's in the balance in the seesaw and I was more weight than Raul and we still get balanced because the placement.
Rich:	Well we still balanced because the placement…
Tammy:	Maybe because of the distance.
Student:	The distance.
Steven:	It's the placement.
Qing:	The placement and the weight.
Student:	Yeah, it's the weight and the placement.

Qing raised an important point in her challenge. By Day 6, the students had begun to coordinate weight and distance as factors that work together to explain balance. However, Tammy's theory was based on just one factor, weight. Qing immediately challenged this theory, with other students joining in to discuss the importance of both factors. As this discussion ended, Raul was encouraged by Mrs. Glenda to make a point that was on his mind.

Raul:	Wait a minute, I have something to say, Qing one they're the one well [interrupts himself].
Mrs. Glenda:	Say it, say it.
Raul:	They're the ones who.
Qing:	But I was disagree.

Mrs. Glenda:	Yeah I know but he's, say what you were gonna say, they're the ones that are supposed to do what?
Raul:	***They're the ones who are supposed to be reporting, you're not the ones who are supposed to be telling what you did, they're supposed to be giving their results.***
Carson:	Emma Emma has to go home at 2:30.
Mrs. Glenda:	Ok, Emma goodbye, stop for just one second, that's an excellent point and maybe that's a point of confusion in here, listen your questions are supposed to get them to tell their theory, [many children start talking at once -there is a heated discussion that is hard to tease apart] you can disagree with their theory.

Raul, as a member of the audience just like Qing, reminded the class that the purpose of audience questions was to allow the reporters to share their ideas and findings with the class. In his view, this was not a time for sharing one's own group results. Mrs. Glenda echoed Raul's contribution noting that questions were designed to get the reporters to share their theories and thinking with the class. It was okay to disagree with them, but the point was to get them to share their ideas. This marked a fascinating point in the development of the community. As the students began building more confidence in their theories and their roles of questioners, they also wanted to discuss and debate the differences that existed between them. On Day 5, they began this process of debate by testing Denise's group's new theory after Rich's challenge. Qing was picking up on this shift in conversational practice in the classroom. She wanted to share her group's finding and theoretical rationale with the class too. There continued to be ambivalence about when and how sharing one's own ideas during the report of another group was permissible. Understanding others ideas and sharing one's own reaction to those ideas, were ongoing and essential aspects of the classroom dialogue.

Day 10: "Nuh uh, it's not equal." On Day 10, Raul and Qing were reporting for their group about making a bridge and then testing it to see how many washers it could hold without collapsing (see Investigation #8, p. 38). This group claimed that they made their bridge with equal length supports and reinforcements and then distributed washers on the bridge equally as well while testing what it could hold. Rich questioned these claims. His challenges drove the conversation for about 10–15 minutes. The discussion began with Rich challenging the claim that the structure itself was symmetrical and built with equal supports.

Raul: We predicted that our structure would hold up the whole box [of washers] and our theory to why it was gonna hold up the whole box of washers was because with all the tape and the way we put the straws um...

Qing: It's all equal.

Rich: **Nuh uh it's not equal.**

Qing: I mean like everything has like that side has three and that side has three like that.

Rich: Nuh uh.

Raul: And these there's these two long, well actually there's four long straws down in the middle which forms like a tipi like the structure of the one we just did [built] yesterday but and those are pushing against the bottom which is holding up the rest with tape and there's other ones attached to that which are attached to other things which attach to other things [some kids laugh] which hold up the washers, yes Rich.

Rich: Well it's not [he walks over to the structure and begins to point].

Raul: Please Rich please! [Rich is close to touching the structure].

Rich: This side goes out more than that side and right down here that sticks out and that sticks out farther.

Qing: [walks over to where the structure is sitting on the table, Rich is still there] That's not really

Raul:	We made it can you please please please please I don't want it to collapse after all that.
Mrs. Glenda:	Hey, Rich Rich, away from the table.
Raul:	See we couldn't make it exactly equal.
Qing:	It can't be perfect too.
Carson:	One little straw is off so everybody makes a big deal.
Rich:	Two straws.
Steven:	So it doesn't have to be perfect.
Raul:	And our results were that it did hold up the whole box of washers.
Rich:	Well them ain't washers anyway, some of them are nuts.

This general conversation, largely directed by Rich's challenges, lasted another few minutes. The students were concerned that Rich was going to knock down their structure after their hard work. They were also critical of his challenges, saying that he was pointing out minor flaws that amounted to very small differences. Mrs. Glenda concluded this group's report by suggesting to the class that perhaps there is a fine line between being "detail oriented" and "nit-picky."

Mrs. Glenda:	I think they did an excellent job, you know what Rich, I understand what you are doing, you are getting really detail oriented, like it would make you happier if they were saying that they put washers and nuts on there, and it would make you happier if...
Rich:	[interrupts Mrs. Glenda] They said it wasn't exactly equal.
Mrs. Glenda:	Yeah, but you know something though, *I mean I understand being so precise but I think I'd like to take Carson's point over there, I mean there's a point where it could be nit picking maybe just a little bit too much, ok but that's for you guys to decide,* I think that you did a terrific job.

Here the students and Mrs. Glenda explicitly discussed the need to differentiate legitimate challenges over essential details versus empty arguing about things that ultimately made little difference in the overall scientific theories or findings.

Challenging was a complex practice in the classroom, one that required careful structuring and explicit discussion to manage and shape into a productive activity. Challenges allowed important intellectual work and social dynamics to be examined by the class.

Being Wrong (and/or Changing One's Mind)

Like challenging, admitting that you were wrong and that you changed your mind was another powerful way of being and knowing that was enacted and discussed over the course of the study. Defensiveness about being wrong was sometimes linked to challenges by another student. Other times it was a spontaneous admission that prompted revised thinking. In the examples provided below, Denise, Qing, and Rich played central roles in bringing about conversations around "being wrong" and how it would be handled in the classroom.

Baseline Day: "They were right but I was wrong." On the baseline day, Denise and Olivia reported about the first balance scale problem on which their group had worked, two 10-gram weights on number 5 on the right side and three 10-gram weights on number 5 on the left side (see Investigation #1, p. 36). Denise did not hesitate to admit that, unlike her group mates who predicted correctly, the prediction she made did not coincide with the results.

Olivia:	I think it will go left and it did.
Denise:	I thought it would balance.
Mrs. Glenda:	You thought it would balance.
Olivia:	Carson [inaudible].
Denise:	Can I see your book Carson, can I see your book? [both Denise and Olivia have their hands out toward Carson]
Mrs. Glenda:	Can they use your data, that's what they're asking, can they read your results, if you don't want to share can they at least read? Can you pass it down.

Denise:	I said it would balance and Carson said it would, he said it would go to the left.
Olivia:	He said the left is gonna go down and the right is gonna go up.
Denise:	**They were right but I was wrong**.
Mrs. Glenda:	That's ok, do you guys, can you tell me why you thought that would happen?

Olivia and Denise announced their predictions to the class and then asked Carson for his notebook so that they could report his results. Olivia shared his predictions. Then Denise announced to the class that Carson and Olivia were right and she was wrong. Mrs. Glenda backed this up directly with "that's okay," and immediately asked the students why they made their predictions. She acknowledged that "being wrong" was ok. And, she wanted the students to think about the deeper question of WHY they were making their predictions and not to be so focused on whether their predictions were right or wrong. Denise's move was very unusual in a school context. Students understand that "being right" is the goal in school, so to admit that one was "wrong" can pose significant challenges for a student. That is why Denise's response on this first day of the study was so unusual. She confidently reported that she did not get something correct whereas all the other students in her group did. This turned out to be a crucial beginning marking Denise's ability to powerfully use her own self-evaluations to significantly develop her own thinking and set an emotional orientation around "being wrong" for the class. Denise served as a model for the class, a model that Mrs. Glenda could emphasize and highlight.

Day 5: "Mrs. Glenda does make mistakes." In the next short example, with Denise's help, Mrs. Glenda positioned herself as someone who makes mistakes. This example took place during the time that they were constructing the Questions Chart together (see Figure 3, p. 92 for a more elaborate description of the Questions Chart).

| Denise: | You made a [spelling] mistake on results. |
| Mrs. Glenda: | **Mrs. Glenda does make mistakes** [said as she corrected the mistake]. |

This exchange is significant because it created an opportunity for Mrs. Glenda to associate herself with Denise and Denise's attention to making and owning mistakes. She happily received Denise's feedback and positions herself just as Denise had done to herself on prior days – as a person who makes mistakes.

Day 5: "I didn't find it but I figured it out from the wrong results." Later on Day 5, Denise articulated, with Mrs. Glenda's help, that she formed a new theory because her previous theories did not help her explain her results. She had presented her new theory, "just double the weight against the distance" and the students asked questions (see pages 123–125 for an earlier description of this moment). Tammy's question below was a first – no one had framed the idea of relating predictions, theories, and findings in quite the same way before. Even Mrs. Glenda seemed impressed.

Tammy:	Where do you find your theory in your findings?
Mrs. Glenda:	Whoa.
Dai:	In the [inaudible].
Comment:	There is a pause in the conversation for about 20 seconds. Mrs. Glenda whispers to Denise to help her understand Tammy's question.
Denise:	*I didn't find it but I figured it out from the wrong results*.
Rich:	The wrong results?
Mrs. Glenda:	When she she thought it was gonna happen one way and ...
Raul:	From the mistake.
Mrs. Glenda:	She figured it out from the mistake. That's exactly right.

Denise, Raul, and Mrs. Glenda helped the other students understand that it was Denise's mistaken prediction that helped her re-evaluate and change her theory. Denise transformed her "being wrong" into a productive counterexample that could propel her theorizing further than it had gone before (see Karmiloff-Smith & Inhelder, 1974). In the process, Denise demonstrated that being wrong had a positive impact on the development of her ideas. This is a central epistemological feature of scientific reasoning that was squarely rooted in a particular way of being as well. Here Denise intentionally and courageously framed her initial ideas as "wrong" and then used her self-evaluation to push her theoretical ideas to change and better explain the unexpected results.

Day 6: "I can say something wrong." The next excerpt from Day 6 showed that admissions of being wrong were not always made under circumstances of self-reflection and reconsidering theories in small groups. Sometimes mistakes were made during the course of presenting ideas to the whole class. Other students pointed out these mistakes. This could lead to defensiveness on the part of the mistaken student. In this report, Qing was reporting for her group about the soda straw balance activity (see Investigation #6, p. 37). The group was confused about how many paper clips they placed on either side of their soda straw balance because they did not keep a good record in their laboratory notebooks.

Qing:	I think the left will go down because they have the same weight.
Dai:	No no no no.
Student:	That doesn't make any sense.
Qing:	[uses her notebook to talk about what they thought] The first one we put was, wait, blah blah blah blah [some students laugh] because because the left hand side have more weight, because we put two I think we put two paper clip on the left and one paper clip on the right, I guess.
Dai:	Ok, um, I think um, you said the um, your theory is um because of the [inaudible] . . .
Qing:	Well, because um I disagree, because the because the left hand side more weight.
Dai:	Well I think I think . . .
Rich:	You just said they had equal weight.
Student:	Yeah you just said . . .

Qing:	People have wrong! [drops her lab book onto the floor]
Mrs. Glenda:	Ok, slow down,
Qing:	*I can say something wrong.*
Mrs. Glenda:	Qing it's ok, you know what, I think…
Student:	It's confusing.
Mrs. Glenda:	Excuse me, I think, if you guys use this also this might help you also [referring to the theory chart recording theories from previous days] I think Dai heard theory number three, is that…
Dai:	Yeah.
Mrs. Glenda:	Is that the theory you think she's working with?

Qing's report was confusing to the students in the audience. Dai restated what he thought she said to try to resolve the inconsistencies in what the audience heard. Qing challenged Dai's recounting and then the other students began to explicitly point out what she had said that was different from what she was now claiming in her challenge. This made Qing defensive and upset. Challenging others' ideas was not a good strategy to move thinking forward in this case. It set up an emotional climate that shut down thinking and communication. Mrs. Glenda immediately mediated the interaction between Qing and Dai. She redirected the conversation to the theory chart, a productive and jointly understood textual reference point, to rescue a conversation that was quickly unraveling. This move is similar to those in writing workshop, where the critical attention is placed on the text and not on the author (see Graves, 1983). Although challenges hold the possibility for productive revision of thinking, they also carry the possibility that someone feels personally attacked as this example and the next also demonstrated.

Day 7: *"This is not an inquisition, so if somebody makes a mistake up there, instead of jumping down their throat…"* On Day 7, Qing was assigned to be reporter for her group again. She reported about balance scale problems. There was tension in the room that mounted on this day as Qing once again made a mistake in reporting the number of grams on one side of the balance scale. Steven, Qing's group member, kept trying to point this out to her. Her mistake supported Rich to argue that her findings were wrong. In addition, earlier in the conversation Rich objected to the fact that Qing said she "knew" something when she should have been reporting a prediction. He said to her, "you can't know you hafta predict." Mrs. Glenda stopped the conversation when it became so heated that she felt it was unproductive. This time there was no way to redirect attention to a jointly created, publicly understood document. She intervened to explicitly talk the students through epistemological and ontological issues that were simmering in the classroom.

Qing:	That's supposed to be 40 [grams on the balance scale].
Steven:	That's what I was trying to tell her.
Qing:	Forty, my fault, ok?
Steven:	Mrs. G, that's what I was trying to tell her.
Qing:	My fault, ok, my fault.
Steven:	I've got four [10 gram weights].
Mrs. Glenda:	Ok, can we just stop for a second?
Steven:	Yeah.
Mrs. Glenda:	Rich turn around, Steven turn around, this is like way too heated, way too heated, if somebody makes a mistake however...
Qing:	I didn't.
Mrs. Glenda:	[interrupts] No listen, if it's one gram weight but it's still working in the theory you should give that person a little bit more respect than you're giving them, I mean I think that it's great that you guys are asking questions and that's what I want you to do, but there is a way to phrase a question so that you're not frying the person that's up there, I mean, I listen [interrupts herself, some students giggle] no, it's not funny, I'm listening to Qing's voice and the pitch is changing, people are getting upset.

Olivia:	Confused.
Mrs. Glenda:	Their feelings are getting hurt, that is not the purpose of this, absolutely not the purpose of this, the purpose is to ask questions to clarify so you get an explanation that you understand, ***this is not an inquisition, so if somebody makes a mistake up there instead of jumping down their throat***, which is what I see going on here, I think what you need to do and which is what I was trying to say to you, there are ways to ask questions to people, you could have said, gee I thought that I heard you say that you had um the ten gram weight on number four, did I did I misunderstand you, that's that's a way of getting them to think back on their procedure without saying you know, in your face, you were wrong.
Rich:	[repeats] In your face [giggles] ...
Mrs. Glenda:	And I think I think what we need to do is kinda calm this down again so that it isn't a circus up here.
Qing:	I can make a real like, we can write over there and no one like we don't yell and ...
Mrs. Glenda:	Yeah I could do that Qing but you know something, you guys are fourth graders do I hafta do that?
Qing:	I just I just don't like people saying nuh uh.
Mrs. Glenda:	Right.
Rich:	You say that too so ...
Mrs. Glenda:	Excuse me, this is exactly what I'm saying.
Steven:	She ain't talkin' to you.
Qing:	You say it first too.
Raul:	Wait shush, you guys are getting angry at each other for no reason.
Mrs. Glenda:	Right.
Raul:	Just stop.

Rich:	I don't get angry at her.
Mrs. Glenda:	I think that there is an important point to this, if you guys would turn around and look at me for just a second, ok, I see two things going on, two things, Richard, if you'll turn around I'm not talkin' to the back of your head, ok, first of all, we've gotten to the point that, when you first started these things, these activities on balance, this is the last round of activities on balance, when you guys started these, you were making predictions and you weren't quite sure, ok, so when you said my prediction was, I thought, I guessed, you guys really meant that, now what's happening is here people are getting up there and they're instead of saying I think, I guess, I hope.
Rich:	[interrupts] They're saying I know!
Mrs. Glenda:	They're saying things like I know, and some people in the audience are getting mad at that, they shouldn't be getting mad at that. Basically what's happened is you've moved to the point where...
Rich:	[interrupts] You don't even think no more!
Mrs. Glenda:	You don't even think about the prediction anymore because you know what's gonna happen right? You pretty much know your theory, that's a wonderful point to be at, that means you guys understand a whole lot more than you did at the beginning.
Student:	All right.

This was the most heated exchange in the study, with hurt feelings and Qing's suggestion that the class write rules for behavior on a poster. The students and Mrs. Glenda were upset with Rich and his approach to handling his disagreement with Qing. Rich did not seem as upset about Qing's mistake in reporting her balance scale problem. Throughout this interaction, it became clear that he had been bothered by Qing's assertion that she "knows" what will happen. As

Mrs. Glenda began talking, Rich joined her in co-constructing his concern. His response (that students were no longer thinking) helped to explain his determination to push his own perspective, even when dealing with the minor mistake of reporting the number of grams in a balance problem. Rich's concerns were crucial and marked a keen sensitivity to an epistemological shift that the other students seemed to have experienced but may not have been able to articulate. Mrs. Glenda thought she understood what Rich's objection was really about. She took this opportunity to address the development in the students' predicting over time – beginning with educated guesses without any theoretical grounding and evolving into theoretically based hypothesizing. But at the same time, she emphasized a way of setting an emotional tone – "a way to phrase a question so that you're not frying the person that's up there." This process of becoming a student of science was marked by significant changes in students' ways of knowing, doing, and being, putting to use these epistemologies through productive modes of interaction with others. Acting with intention, Rich pushed this agenda. He often embodied extraordinary ways of knowing (for a fourth grader) but packaged this in ways of being that irritated even his most patient classmates.

As this chapter has proceeded, we moved from new ways of knowing, being, and doing that were engaged by the large majority of students in the class. Negotiating speaking rights and persisting in the face of difficulty to understand and articulate ideas were things that all students took up, some more than others. However, taking perspectives, challenging ideas, and being wrong were frequent strategies of a smaller group of students in the class. This raises the question about the personal trajectories of the individual students within this new community. We turn to this lens in Chapter 4 as we seek to examine individual student's experiences across the duration of the study.

4   Personal Lens of Analysis

Individual Learning Trajectories

> For whatever the art, the science, the literature, the history, and the geography of a culture, each man must be his own artist, his own scientist, his own historian, his own navigator. No person is master of the whole culture; indeed, this is almost a defining characteristic of that form of social memory that we speak of as culture. Each man lives a fragment of it. To be whole, he must create his own version of the world, using that part of his cultural heritage he has made his own through education.
>
> (Bruner, 1962, p. 116)

Our analyses now turn to catching students in the act of making their culture their own through their experiences in Mrs. Glenda's science classroom. In this chapter we plot students' evolution over time as they created and negotiated concepts and epistemological practices together with the emotional climate and distinctions of worth within their classroom. Students brought their own "history in person" (Holland, Lachicotte, Skinner, & Cain, 1998) as a starting point for improvising in this new classroom context.

We met the students at the classroom door and got to know them more through interviews and Mrs. Glenda's reflections. We had limited information about students' experiences in other classrooms and contexts outside of school. We followed how each student interacted with the new values and practices that were being introduced in the context of the study classroom. Through these case studies, we show how four students learned and emerged as contributors to the quality and vitality of the classroom community. We address the following questions: *What ways of being, knowing, and doing do individual students espouse and what patterns of interaction do students enact at the beginning of the classroom experience? How do individual students' initial ways of knowing, interests, motivations, and affective orientations toward learning change across the duration of the classroom experience? How do the students talk about and reflect on their own participation in the classroom?*

All of the students in the class have their own stories to tell. We have learned from each one. Because a full treatment of all cases would constitute an entire book, we focus on four condensed cases in this chapter. We share cases of Rich, Denise, Raul, and Christie. The focal students were selected for multiple reasons. First, we wanted to select students who would represent key social categories including sex and ethnic and racial groups (see Table 1, p. 31). Second, we wanted students at varying levels of questioning in the class (see Figure 2, p. 51). Raul represents a student who was a higher than average questioner, Denise was an average questioner, Rich was just below the average, and Christie was in the bottom three questioners in the class. When possible, we based our analyses on interviews with Mrs. Glenda and the students and classroom transcripts to plot each student's experience over the course of the study. Because Chapters 2 and 3 involve extensive use of key pieces of transcript from the classroom, in this chapter we will refer back to students' personal participation in those interpersonal interactions that contributed to the creation of a community climate for learning. We will also include new segments of transcript that were not used in prior chapters to attend to the personal experiences of focal students.

Interviews were conducted with a subset of participating students. Rich, Raul, and Christie were all interviewed but Denise was not. The interviews were not conceptualized as a main part of the initial study. They asked about students' perspectives on thinking like scientists but they did not ask for students' reflection about emotional experiences and valued ways of being in the classroom. As a result, in some cases the interviews are of limited value for the current purpose of understanding the broad view of learning we are investigating. Nonetheless, when relevant issues did emerge spontaneously in the interviews, they were illuminating, providing further insight into students' personal experiences in the classroom.

Each case will begin with a description of the student followed by a timeline of their personal learning trajectory over the course of the study. We will use these timelines to plot the way each student contributed to the ways of knowing, doing, and being in the class across time. The timeline will be followed by a more in-depth analysis of the episodes captured in the timeline. Each focal student's learning opportunities and the possibilities each student provided for other students' learning are discussed. We begin this intra-personal analysis with Rich.

Rich

Rich was a "neighborhood kid," assigned to the magnet school where the study took place not because a parent or guardian selected it but because it was the closest public school. He was a lower-socioeconomic status (SES) European-American boy. Mrs. Glenda reported that he was undergoing special testing at the time of the study to ensure that the school provided adequate emotional and behavioral support for him. She talked about how she came to know Rich as a kindergartener years before the study began.

> *Mrs. Glenda:* When Rich was in kindergarten he and a friend broke all the windows in his house. They just threw rocks through all the windows in the house and he lost recess for a year. And, that was the year that instead of doing [lunch] duties, I contracted out to be recess Gestapo. So anybody who was bad, they were supposed to come down to the library and sit with me, like I'm really big punishment [Leslie laughs with Mrs. Glenda]. And Rich and his friend spent the whole year with me.

In effect, Rich spent lunch recess of his first year of public schooling in detention. He was 5 years old and behaving in ways that identified him as a child "at risk" of developing more behavioral issues as he got older. Mrs. Glenda laughed as she told the story because although she realized the official purpose of the detention was to punish Rich and his friend, she did not view herself nor was she viewed by the students themselves as "punishment." Mrs. Glenda first developed her relationship with Rich in this setting, one where she came to appreciate him as a person. Because Mrs. Glenda knew that Rich's current and prior behavior could be challenging, she did not expect things in the study classroom to be any different. As a special education teacher, this was not a problem for her. She liked Rich and felt that he had the ability to engage in "science talk" right from the beginning of the study. At one point, she spontaneously reflected on Rich's capabilities after Day 3.

Mrs. Glenda: The two [students] who understand it [balance scale problems] the most intuitively are Carson and Rich.

Leslie: Why [do you think that]?

Mrs. Glenda: Rich wasn't satisfied that it was just weight and it bugged him that nobody [in his small group] mentioned distance. He knew the group [his small group] wasn't giving a complete theory. Yet, if you got him up there [to report in front of the class], he wouldn't sound like the most knowledgeable source in the room. But there is just this intuitive, whatever, that he does understand. Often times it's not verbal, it's not public.

Mrs. Glenda put her finger on something she noticed early on about Rich – he had an "intuitive" grasp of the phenomenon that he sometimes had difficulty communicating to others. He noticed things and worked hard to share his thinking, although in this case it made no difference in his group's report. His group, all girls except for Rich, ignored his attempts to participate in creating their report for Day 3. The girls were writing theories focused on weight and did not account for distance from the fulcrum. This bothered Rich. From Mrs. Glenda's point of view, Rich was engaged in deep thinking and was trying to be a part of the ongoing work of the classroom.

When interviewed after Day 3 of the study, Rich was asked what he liked about science classes with Mrs. Glenda. His reply provided a window into his perspective on the social-emotional dimensions of the classroom.

> *Rich:*   No one's always wrong and no one's always right. If I do something wrong, I don't really get in trouble and people they like to, they already know that I sometimes have trouble in the group. Sometimes they know how to get me back in a group. So we could all be cooperating.

Rich's comments foreground correctness, with respect to curricular content and moral responsibility in the classroom. He liked the fact that students were not consistently viewed as either "right" or "wrong" with respect to their intellectual ideas and behavior. His comment points to opportunities for revision and change as central features of his experience in Mrs. Glenda's classroom. He positioned himself as someone who could "do something wrong" and then re-evaluate this with the assistance of his peers. He did not "get in trouble" but his group had a chance to help get him to work with them again so that they could all cooperate together. These reflections suggest that Rich liked the sense that things could change and that he could be a part of that change.

As we look across Rich's timeline, he was at the center of several key changes in the classroom. He was instrumental in Mrs. Glenda's initial efforts to support students to take on the role of questioners in the classroom (Day 3). Rich also initiated intellectual discussions around "Denise's theory," the first approach that coordinated weight and distance from the fulcrum as important factors that explain balance (Day 5). Finally, Rich was the impetus for several discussions that centered on expectations for the emotional climate in the classroom (Days 4, 7, 10). Rich was outspoken and that proved extremely helpful in the early days of supporting other students to learn to question. However, Rich's outspokenness often took the form of challenges. Challenging offered opportunities for the class to discuss important intellectual ideas but also raised issues about how to deliver a challenge that were important for Rich and his classmates to engage. Rich had to learn to temper his enthusiasm and know when to offer his ideas and when to allow other students to speak

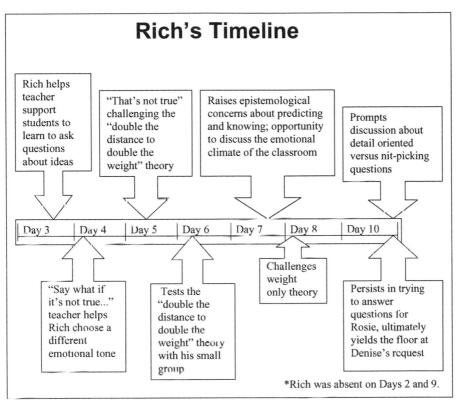

Figure 5. Rich's Timeline Across Instruction.

for themselves. He also had to learn strategies for sharing his ideas that would be less likely to annoy and more likely to engage his classmates. Rich learned through his classroom interactions and also offered his classmates learning opportunities that may not have been available to them had Rich not been in this classroom. These opportunities for learning focused on essential ways of knowing in science and effective ways of being a skeptic, something that is a prized value for students of science (Rutherford & Ahlgren, 1990).

Questioning and Challenging

Although Rich reported having difficulties working in his small group on Day 3, he emerged as a capable questioner of reporters early in the study. The role he played in questioning and challenging was evident in the analyses presented in Chapters 2 and 3. In those chapters, we explored how students took up the role of questioning one another and how this new questioning practice had a ripple effect inciting additional practices that distinguish the study classroom from typical elementary school classrooms. Rich's participation in the questioning routine on Day 3 provided Mrs. Glenda with the opportunity to move from teacher to peer modeling of questioning strategies. It was a key transition to students' fully assuming the role of questioning each other.

Rich's facility in asking questions may have contributed to another regular feature of his classroom interaction – *challenges*. He was the most frequent challenger in the classroom, initiating 59 percent of the challenges across the course of the study. Qing and Raul were the only other students who participated in this practice. Rich's challenging episodes were accompanied by some of the most intellectually engaging and productive questioning in the class. The other students clarified and discussed Rich's questions and challenges. At times, however, they also began to treat Rich as if he had a predilection for being disagreeable and disruptive. His emotional orientation could be viewed as confrontational or dismissive and his posture was often doggedly persistent. Mrs. Glenda knew that Rich's thinking and approach were vital to the classroom and that he brought an intuition about the content that was not always apprehended by his classmates. She worked to draw out his strengths to support his and other students' deliberation about important conceptual and epistemological issues. His behavior surfaced important issues with respect to emotional climate and distinctions of worth in the classroom. Mrs. Glenda used these opportunities to reflect on how and why one might want to ask questions of others to encourage productive discussion rather than empty arguing. Rich was often at the center of the best instructional conversations in the classroom with respect to ways of knowing and doing, as well as ways of being.

Challenging and Revising Thinking

Rich also learned to better understand and explain balance through his participation in the classroom. His challenges sparked his own reflection and thinking about coordinating weight and distance from the fulcrum to explain balance. It helped him build a better way to communicate what he intuitively seemed to understand as early as Day 3 – that weight and distance from the fulcrum were important factors to explain the behavior of the balance scale. Rich's initial knee-jerk reaction was to challenge Denise's group's theory ("you can double the distance on one side to double the weight on the other") on Day 5. He focused intently on the debate that followed and was convinced that maybe Denise had found a way to communicate what he had been trying to say to his group all along, that both weight and distance from the fulcrum mattered. His own group member, Rosie, remained unconvinced of the theory's utility, so on Day 6 Rich and his small group created other problems with Mrs. Glenda's assistance to put the theory to multiple tests. In this setting, Rich became the champion of the "double the distance to double the weight" theory. Rich was pleased that they were able to confirm the theory's explanatory value with repeated trials. This was a remarkable accomplishment for Rich and his group, given Chinn and Brewer's (1993) research that suggests that students do not commonly change theories in the face of disconfirming evidence.

Respectful Challenging

On Day 7, Rich challenged Qing's group and raised an epistemo-logical concern. Qing asserted when she reported her prediction that she "knew" what would happen. Rich was not happy about that and said, "you can't *know* it, you hafta *predict*." As a result of Rich's questioning, Qing eventually offered a theory to support her pre-dictions. She provided the multiplicative rule of torque arguing that one must multiply the weight times the distance on each side of the fulcrum to allow comparison across the arms of the balance scale. This moved beyond the contextually specific "double the distance to double the weight" theory suggested by Denise's group and further tested by Rich's small group. Rich continued to challenge Qing, who had reported the distance from the fulcrum incorrectly for one of the balance scale problems she discussed, which further complicated the interaction. The conversation continued until it was clear that the students were frustrated with Rich's persistence. Mrs. Glenda stopped the conversation and intervened to talk to the students about the tone and delivery of their questions. She emphasized that seeing students ask questions was amazing but that there was a way to ask questions "so that you're not frying the person that's up there." This was the most explicit and heated discussion about the emotional climate in the classroom. They were setting expectations for respectful interaction with one another that would further support productive discussion and debate of the intellectual ideas.

Immediately following these comments, Mrs. Glenda went back to what she thought was motivating Rich's entrenchment – his initial statement to Qing, "you can't *know* you hafta *predict*." As Mrs. Glenda began to address this issue, Rich interrupted and argued that the students were not thinking anymore. Rich's concerns were crucial and marked a keen sensitivity to an epistemological shift that the other students seemed to have experienced but may not have been able to articulate.[1] Mrs. Glenda took this opportunity to address the development in the students' predicting over time – which began with educated guesses without any theoretical grounding and evolved into theoretically based hypothesizing. This was a remarkable accomplishment in the classroom ways of knowing. It was something Mrs. Glenda had an opportunity to explicitly address and celebrate thanks to Rich's persistence. However, the other students were upset with him. When he made a bid to ask another question during the report, the other students let him know that he was not giving others a turn and that he was getting them "off-track." They sent Rich a direct message in connection to the ways of being in the classroom. There were more appropriate approaches to use in getting topics on the floor that would respect the web of values and socio-scientific norms that they had created in this classroom context. He needed to join the class and respect these values.

This theme about how to ask respectful questions was built upon further on Day 10 when Rich challenged again. The students were reporting about making a bridge and testing it to see how many

---

[1] Perhaps Rich noticed this because he did not understand Qing's multiplicative theory. However, many other students also seemed to have difficulty understanding Qing's theory but did not comment on her use of "know" versus "think" or "predict."

washers it could hold without collapsing. Raul and his group claimed that they made their bridge with "equal" length supports and reinforcements and then distributed washers on the bridge while testing what it could hold. Rich questioned these claims. His challenges directed the conversation for about 10–15 minutes. Carson, an audience member, commented, "one little straw is off so everybody makes a big deal." Mrs. Glenda picked up on his comment and suggested that there is a fine line between being "detail oriented" and "nitpicky." This conversation represented a real respect for Rich's perspective. Mrs. Glenda and students engaged his ideas fully over a good bit of class time. It also marked a willingness to explicitly provide Rich with feedback about his challenging behavior. They did this respectfully without putting Rich on the spot and making him defensive. They expected him to do the same.

Later on this day, the episode with which we opened the book took place. Denise made an incredibly sophisticated social move that provided feedback to Rich as well as opened up the floor for Rosie to share her ideas. Rich continued to assert his own view about his group's theory even after Denise made it clear that she was interested to hear what she thought was a different theory being offered by Rosie. Denise eventually had to get very direct with Rich, telling him "I heard your theory – now I want to hear Rosie's." Rich finally stopped talking for his group when Denise said this to him. He was learning how to take feedback and when to allow other students to speak for themselves.

Essential discussions in this classroom would not have been possible without Rich. However, it was evident that the interactions were sometimes difficult for the students and Mrs. Glenda. Rich had clear strengths. Whereas other students struggled to learn how to ask questions of others, Rich did this effortlessly. His emotional orientation, however, was often confrontational and argumentative. As a result, other students viewed Rich as disagreeable and disrespectful at times. Yet, the students listened to his ideas and accepted what he offered, even if his ideas were shrouded in a general stubbornness. His challenging behavior offered important learning opportunities for his classmates. On most occasions, Rich's challenges drew careful intellectual responses from his peers rather than attempts to shut him down. Rich became the skeptic, externalizing doubts and alternatives for the others, and pressing things that they might want to consider more before clinging too tightly to their theoretical points of view. He became the Piagetian "social other" that students could use as a foil to build their own understanding (Bearison, 1991; Damon, 1983; Hinde, Perret-Clermont, & Stevenson-Hinde, 1985; Piaget, 1970; Rogoff, 1990). In responding to this important intellectual voice, the students also had to discern when his perspective had substance and when it was focused on trivial details that took attention away from the "big picture." It was important that the students came to appreciate and evaluate the merits of Rich's challenges. This allowed the class to see that although challenges could push thinking forward, they did not always required one to revise thinking. Some challenges could be discussed and discarded as irrelevant under certain conditions. Other issues could be discarded because they met the criteria of "nit-picking" and not foundational, relevant issues that contribute to underlying explanations of phenomena.

On a social-emotional level, Rich presented opportunities to others to find ways to make disagreement a positive rather than a negative aspect of their classroom conversations. Instead of viewing Rich as a "worst offender" who violated unspoken "civility laws" in the classroom (see Graff, 1992; Wineburg & Grossman, 2001), they had to see the merit in his ideas while also explicitly commenting on his tone, word choice, tendency to put people on the defensive, and attempts to speak for others. Rich provided many opportunities for everyone to reflect on how they were becoming students of science and what values and beliefs they would bring to their collective work. These findings suggest that Rich "composed a life" (Bateson, 1990) for himself within this new classroom community, improvising in ways that contributed to his own learning and to that of others in the classroom.

Denise

Denise was an African American student from a lower SES background. She did not participate in interviews during the study but was very willing to share her opinion and perspective with Mrs. Glenda.

The spontaneous comments she made to Mrs. Glenda throughout the study were important windows into her experience in the classroom. From the beginning, Denise was an active participant who took initiative in presenting problems and assisting students. On the baseline day, Denise volunteered to report for her group whereas other members of her group refused. Denise courageously explained several balance scale problems in front of a class of some unfamiliar students and a new teacher (she had not worked with Mrs. Glenda before this class). Denise already showed the capacity and interest to take responsibility as a spokesperson for her group and an inclination to be a dynamic part of her surroundings. After the baseline, Mrs. Glenda commented on Denise's behavior in her small group and during her report saying, "you know what is interesting, you have some really strong girl egos." After Day 2, with more observations and information Mrs. Glenda described Denise again.

Mrs. Glenda:	Denise is a prima donna and is going to moan and groan the entire way through...it was like what I was saying to you last night. Which end of the funnel you're working from. She'll have to pare down some of her behaviors to work in a group.
Leslie:	She wants to control the group, huh?
Mrs. Glenda:	In every form. Whether it's writing, whether it's talking, or drawing or manipulating materials. She's trying to take over my role too. She's come up to me several times to tell me what she thinks I need to fix and whether or not she should be in charge of this and blah blah blah. So she's kinda the kid you put into the wide end of the funnel and constrain her learning space enough to have her work in a group.

It was clear to Mrs. Glenda from the first day of the study that Denise was a bright and capable student. However, she also had a "big ego" and was trying to take over and do things for other students. She also tried to control the teacher's role by telling Mrs. Glenda how the class should proceed. Mrs. Glenda knew that for Denise to work in a collaborative group, she would need to adjust her behavior to accommodate other students' participation. Later, during the same interview, Mrs. Glenda made this prediction.

> *Mrs. Glenda:*   I think when she [Denise] gets a little less arrogant, she's gonna be crucial in asking questions.

Little did Mrs. Glenda know just how right she was going to be about this prediction. Although Denise developed a reputation for taking over for others at the beginning of the study, this changed across time. She was not the most talkative student in the class. As Figure 2 shows, Denise was active, yet asked questions at an average frequency for the class.

Denise brought a candid and confident demeanor that she used as a basis for improvisation within new classroom values and practices. She was instrumental in discussions about coordinating weight and distance from the fulcrum to explain balance. She also created opportunities for herself and others to value mistakes and "being wrong" as an essential part of the learning process. Finally, she transformed her participation in the classroom, moving from offering to talk for other students to offering opportunities for other students to speak for themselves.

Presenting Key Theoretical Ideas

On Day 5, Denise's thinking came to the fore when she articulated a new theory for the balance scale problems that coordinated weight and distance from the fulcrum as essential elements ("you can double the distance on one side to double the weight on the other"). Mrs. Glenda, witness to Denise's theoretical revision during group work time, deliberately nominated Denise to report on the third step, relating predictions and theories to results because she wanted Denise to articulate her new idea to the class. Denise demonstrated a balance scale problem to illustrate how she came up with her new theory during group work time. Denise's theory triggered an extensive discussion because some students doubted its utility. The students made predictions and came up with theories and argued about their thinking. When Denise completed the demonstration and her

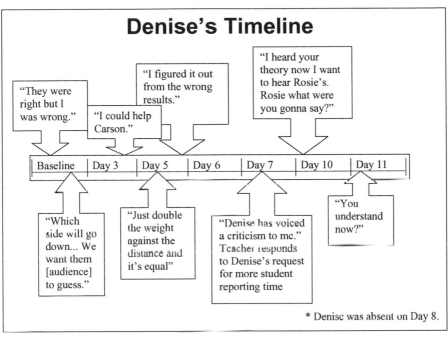

Figure 6. Denise's Timeline Across Instruction.

theory held, there was palpable excitement in the classroom. This day marked a shift to more frequent peer-to-peer interaction, because the development of this new theory happened just as the students began to gain enough experience asking questions. This new theory was also significant to the conceptual learning because up to this point the students' theories focused on either weight or distance as the sole factors that explained the balance scale behavior. Weight and distance from the fulcrum had not yet been integrated into one theory until Denise's new theory was proposed. She was instrumental in bringing this new thinking to the class.

Embracing Being Wrong in the Classroom

Denise played a prominent role in recognizing false predictions and revisiting initial theories to revise them to better explain experimental results. She often talked about this as "being wrong." On the baseline day, Denise spontaneously admitted that her prediction was wrong while Carson's and Olivia's was right. This initial admission gave Mrs. Glenda a chance to establish that being wrong was okay. On Day 5, Denise reported that her group made incorrect predictions and witnessed unexpected results, which led her to develop her new theory. Her erroneous predictions stimulated her thinking and helped her revise her theory. Thanks to Denise's frankness and ease, Mrs. Glenda was able to articulate an important guideline for the class: having false predictions was acceptable, even desirable (Karmiloff-Smith & Inhelder, 1974). Revising theories based on a mismatch between predictions and findings is a critical part of experimental scientific thinking. Denise was the key contributor in bringing this important way of being a science student into the classroom discussion.

On Day 9, Mrs. Glenda explicitly told the students that, "there is never a failure, never" when Dai reported that although they worked hard on their bridge it did not turn out. Denise questioned her saying, "Never?" Mrs. Glenda replied, "Never. Because you can always learn from something." Denise and Mrs. Glenda worked together to create a classroom climate where revising ideas and learning from mistakes was a central value for being a good scientist.

Eliciting Ideas and Participation from Peers

Denise also learned to direct her own interest in leading classroom discussion in a way that invited and motivated other students' participation. On the baseline day, Denise wanted students in the audience to participate in guessing the outcome of balance scale problems. This was an unusual approach. Denise was determined to get responses from her peers as she asked questions three more times and even insisted, with Olivia's help, that everyone listen. She took up the role of teacher as she asked these questions of the audience, choosing to participate in a very different way from most of the other student reporters. Her approach supported her classmates to become more focused on important content and more attentive and involved in her report.

On Day 3, Denise's interest in supporting other students took on a different tone. This was the second day that audience members took on the intellectual audience roles and the students struggled to ask appropriate questions to fulfill these new responsibilities. Carson and Christie were reporters for Denise's group on this day. They had difficulty even beginning their report to the class and stood with their heads down and their eyes focused on the floor. To encourage Carson, Mrs. Glenda scaffolded the situation by having the audience ask questions immediately instead of having Carson proceed with a report. Denise was eager to help and said, "I could help Carson." Mrs. Glenda stopped Denise and reinforced the intellectual audience roles by asking the students responsible for checking predictions and theories to help Carson instead. Mrs. Glenda provided Carson space to express his thinking and prevented other more verbal classmates like Denise from taking over this important speaking role. Carson continued to struggle and Denise jumped in to answer questions. However, when students in the audience said they were not satisfied with their understanding of the group's predictions and theories, Denise said that it was not her report – that she was the scribe. Mrs. Glenda had to intervene again to offer Carson a chance to talk, saying "Denise, Denise it's his job and I just heard him say I don't think I know." Denise's assertiveness was problematic in this case as she was undermining another student's attempts to take on a role that was challenging for him. As Mrs. Glenda supported Carson to develop more confidence in his own abilities to report about his thinking, Denise's attempts to speak for him and to critique the report itself worked contrary to Mrs. Glenda's intentions of providing Carson with a successful reporting experience. In this case, Mrs. Glenda was providing important feedback to both Carson, who needed help learning how to find his voice, and Denise, who needed to know when to allow other students to speak for themselves.

On Day 7, Denise's outspokenness helped her play a pivotal role in negotiating classroom structure for herself and for her peers. Denise had expressed to Mrs. Glenda that students were frustrated because they did not have enough time to report about their activities. It had been a hard day. Denise reported that she did not feel well during the small-group work time. It was hot inside the classroom and the students seemed more agitated and had a much harder time settling into reporting time. Mrs. Glenda had to ask Christie to leave the classroom after she repeatedly refused to pay attention to the reporters. As the reporting period continued and did not improve, Mrs. Glenda stopped the students and brought up Denise's suggestion.

> *Mrs. Glenda:* **"Denise has voiced a criticism to me** and I am gonna honor her criticism, can you move over just a little so I can look at her when I say this, she said that if I spent less time talking in the beginning we'd have more time talking in the end.... You come in and just do your project, well I'll tell you what, how about if we come in and.... Is that ok if we just do reports instead of me talking at all?"

Mrs. Glenda took a harried class moment, to stop and "honor" Denise's criticism of the classroom structure. In this situation, Mrs. Glenda reinforced Denise's competence and authority in establishing classroom structure. Denise expressed an exceptional request. The students were dissatisfied because they wanted *more* time to share their ideas in reporting sessions. Mrs. Glenda agreed to shorten her introductory remarks so that the students could accrue time to report and discuss their ideas together. Denise, as advocate for her classmates, became a catalyst in creating a classroom space that revolved around discussion of students' ideas. She was confident enough to offer this criticism to Mrs. Glenda. Although other students were thinking the same thing and voiced their support after Mrs. Glenda's suggestion, Denise is the student who brought this proposal to Mrs. Glenda's attention.

On Day 10, Denise took up the role of advocating for another student to express a theory that was different from her reporting partner. This is the example that we use in opening the book. Denise used her own confidence and assertiveness to explicitly address Rich's attempt to speak for Rosie. This day contrasted with Day 3 when Denise repeatedly tried to speak for Carson. Denise persisted in asking about Rosie's theory as Rich also repeatedly said he had spoken for their group. Once Denise had successfully offered Rosie the floor, she played a pivotal role in supporting Rosie by asking her questions that helped her express her theory. In contrast to Day 3 when Mrs. Glenda was trying to keep Denise quiet to give Carson the floor, Denise advocated for Rosie and gave her space to think and express herself. Denise combined her assertiveness and confidence with her newfound appreciation for hearing other students' ideas. Denise pursued a key epistemological goal in science – to understanding competing theories. She also joined Mrs. Glenda in creating an emotional climate that valued all students' ideas by offering Rosie an opportunity to present her theory to the class.

During reporting on the last day, Day 11, Denise monitored and supported other students' understanding and offered her fellow group members opportunities to share their thinking. Denise stated the group's prediction and theory about the key concepts of tension and compression when building a tipi (see Investigation #10, p. 39). Steven was confused about this and looked to Mrs. Glenda for an explanation. After Mrs. Glenda's explanation, Denise checked in with Steven by asking, "you understand now?" This was a unique moment because Denise, as Steven's peer, wanted to make sure he understood and did not want to move forward if he was still confused. Later in the same discussion, Denise invited Christie, her reporting partner, to answer questions posed by the audience. Although the students in the audience were directing questions to her, Denise deflected these questions to Christie so that she would have a chance to respond too. Later, Denise asked Emma (a student in the audience) to repeat her group's theory for other students who were having difficulty understanding what tension and compression meant. Denise selected Emma, who rarely volunteered to participate on her own, and invited her into the conversation. Emma responded and began to share her ideas as other students continued to talk. Denise stopped them and said, "I'm having a hard time hearing Emma with everyone else talking." Over the course of the study, Denise transformed her participation from talking for students to offering other students opportunities to speak for themselves while maintaining her own strong voice in the classroom. She used her own forthright and confident manner to improvise and bring about learning opportunities for herself and her classmates.

Denise was instrumental in shaping the classroom community and the dialogue that unfolded over time. She played a key emergent role within this classroom, positioning herself as a kind of "junior teacher" from the baseline day. At first she seemed to conceptualize this role as one of unwavering authority, where she had a chance to do things for other students during small-group time. She also asked students questions for which she knew the answers and assessed their responses during whole-class reporting. However, as time went on, Denise's orientation to her self-appointed junior teacher role seemed to change. She became more familiar with the ways of thinking like a scientist and the audience roles where distributed thinking had to happen as a norm across all students in the classroom. She also had a chance to watch Mrs. Glenda's example that provided her with a new model of what a teacher might do and say in a classroom. Like an architect responsible for creating physical spaces, Denise created intellectual and social spaces that promoted learning. Her confidence that permitted her to admit to "being wrong" and her move to offer other students' opportunities to share their thinking deeply affected the learning. Denise's presence in this class offered opportunities for everyone to learn new ways of knowing, doing, and being in science.

Raul

Raul was a middle-class bilingual Latino student. He lived in the school's neighborhood and attended the school because his family selected it for him. He was a mature, bright, and verbal student. He stood out because of his tendency to explain, take others' perspectives, clarify ideas, and negotiate with his peers. Raul quickly understood newly presented ideas and often seemed one step ahead of the other students. He was very involved in class activities and discussions. He was one of the top two questioners during whole-class reporting time.

Mrs. Glenda talked about Raul as a capable student who offered strong explanations and always seemed to understand central concepts and ideas. In her reflections after Day 2, she discussed Raul's role as the courageous reporter during the students' first session taking on the audience roles. She said, "it was hard for me not to turn to Raul who had given me this great explanation and not frame it up for him right there on the spot." Mrs. Glenda had to support the students in the audience to do this work, but she found it difficult because Raul provided such a strong explanation. Later that day, she also noted that, "Raul understood the pan balance activity was just a comparison of unequal weights. I don't think the other kids have that at all." Mrs. Glenda often identified Raul as a student who understood things before other students.

When Raul did not understand something, Mrs. Glenda took this as evidence that she needed to provide more support for the students, as on Day 3.

Mrs. Glenda: Like Raul, he just laid down on the rug when I gave him his job card [for the third step of relating predictions and theories to results]. Because Raul knows what he wants to do for step one [predictions and theories] and he probably knows what he needs to do for step two [summarizing results], but I think step three is the hardest. I think maybe what I can do is get some public stuff up there during my orientation...

Raul served as a metric for understanding what to do to best support student learning. When Raul did not understand or seemed frustrated, it was a good indication that other students would feel that way too. He was very verbal and his comments and struggles in class also helped Mrs. Glenda understand how best to support all students' learning.

Over the course of the study, Raul's confidence and ability to explain his ideas served as a basis for improvisation within new classroom values and practices. He was instrumental in helping create joint understanding of key terms and concepts. He also took others' perspectives to help the class discuss conceptual and semantic sticking points. Raul was successful at negotiating interpersonal differences as a result and was a key player in establishing shared understanding in the classroom.

Explanation

Raul came to the classroom with a keen ability to explain and a strong desire to reason through the activities and phenomena under

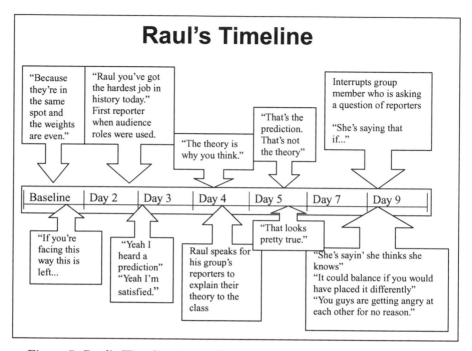

Figure 7. Raul's Timeline Across Instruction.

investigation. Mrs. Glenda became aware of Raul's ability to articulate ideas early in the study and often positioned him to refine explanations and act as a model for the rest of the class. However, sometimes his elaborate explanations would overshadow his group members.

From the first day, Raul took the initiative to answer questions relevant to what was being learned. Students were making predictions about the outcome of balance scale problems. In the midst of student predictions, Mrs. Glenda stepped into the discussion and said she "would be interested to know why." Raul replied immediately saying, "because they're in the same spot and the weights are even." Raul often answered questions before his peers and offered articulate and relevant explanations. His ability was unusual. Mrs. Glenda used Raul's early explanations to support the class, especially in the first few days of the study when other students struggled to express their ideas and ask questions of one another.

On Day 2, Raul took on a leadership role by being the first reporter to present on the first day the intellectual audience roles were implemented in whole-class discussion. Because audience questions would be directed to the reporter, it was a new and possibly intimidating position for a student. This was not a role that was specifically planned for Raul. His group just happened to be the first up for reporting on that first day. Raul reported that in his group Steven had placed 39 grams in one side of the pan balance (see Investigation #4, p. 36). They did not have the weights to match 39 grams on the other side so they put 40 grams in the other pan. Raul reported that he thought it was going to balance because "they were two very close numbers but it didn't balance." He gave a clear and articulate description of the process his group followed as well as the prediction and theory they created. Mrs. Glenda stopped him and asked the students in the audience who were assigned the role of checking predictions and theories to determine if they heard a prediction and a theory presented. Raul endured a long session where Mrs. Glenda worked with students in the audience to support them to learn to monitor their own understanding and to ask questions when they did not understand what someone else said. He turned out to be an exemplary first time reporter for the class. Not only did he provide a strong explanation, he also modeled a way of being positioned so as to answer audience questions without becoming frustrated. Mrs. Glenda reiterated this challenging task in the end by saying, "Raul, you've got the hardest job in history today." On Day 3, when Raul was interviewed about his experiences he mentioned that he would like to pick which job he wanted to do. He said, "I don't like reporter that much. I kinda wish I could trade it for a job that someone else has." Although Raul was successful in this role of reporter, it's obvious from these comments that it was challenging for him. He did have a hard job that day.

On Day 4, even though he was not an assigned reporter, he opted into a discussion to share his small group's theory with the class. His group mates were having difficulty articulating their theory to the class. Steven, one of the reporters, suggested that Raul tell Qing, the other reporter, the theory and then she could share it with the class. Raul did not do this. He shared the theory himself but as he shared Qing participated in representing the ideas with him. Raul welcomed Qing's participation but he effectively took over the job of reporting for his group. This was a dilemma for Raul. He came to the classroom with a strong foundation in answering why and how questions. He was instrumental in providing peer models for thinking and sharing practices. However, he also had a tendency to take over these responsibilities from fellow students. This was especially true of his interactions with his small-group members during reporting. As an audience member Raul often recognized, probed, and responded to other students' ideas (as evidenced in the analyses throughout the next two sections). However, as a small-group member he had a hard time refraining from sharing ideas for his group members.

Days 8 and 9 illustrate Raul's tendencies to support student participation while at times extending his scope of participation to speaking for others. On Day 8, Qing and Steven were due to report. Because Raul wrote the plan for the group, they invited him to participate in reporting this part to the class. Once he was done, Qing reported for their group. During the rest of their report, all three students participated and answered questions from the audience. On Day 9, Qing and Raul each made bids as audience members to ask reporters a question at the same time. Raul forged ahead with his own questions even in the face of Steven telling him two times that he was interrupting Qing. Raul could overshadow other students, especially Qing, with his desire to share his explanations or ask reporters' questions. Qing was the only student who asked more questions than Raul over the course of the study. Both were strong, confident, and frequent participants in the classroom. The familiarity they developed in their small group and Qing's regular participation may have contributed to Raul's willingness to talk over her. Although Raul talked over Qing on occasion in the whole-class format, he shared responsibility for the small-group work and forged deep and lasting new friendships with group members. Raul had to ask Steven his name on the first days of the study, but when interviewed after Day 9 and at the end of the study, Raul asked to invite Steven to talk to Leslie with him so they could share their experiences together. Raul was the only student to put forward this request.

A recurrent theme in Raul's interviews was the role that the science lessons played in helping him explain his ideas. When he and Steven were asked what they liked about how they learned in Mrs. Glenda's class they shared the following:

Raul: She teaches us predicting and stuff which, theory, theories and predictions and we don't do that really in Mrs. Smith's class [his regular classroom]. The only thing we do [in Mrs. Smith's class] is predict what is gonna happen in an experiment. We don't have theories why and stuff like that.

Leslie: Do you like doing it that way, with the predicting and the theories?

Raul: Yeah because it helps. I mean, it helps you talk to another person and tell them more about what you were doing [several other students from the study gather around – the interview is taking place on the playground – and say "yes, yes"].

Steven: Without the questions, we'd be all confused.

Raul: Yeah then we'd just get a strange picture, you might see very clearly because you're the person who did the thing but they don't get it. They get another picture, a different theory in their mind and then when they do the project they get confused and it's just that they maybe think about it different than you would.

Steven: Yeah they get all confused and they get mad because they don't understand it. And, you do more talking [with Mrs. Glenda].

Raul: It's the same amount about talking it's just that the way you talk you can explain it better.

Raul and Steven both discussed the role that theories played in helping them explain their ideas more effectively. Raul described how theories helped surface underlying explanations that could otherwise remain hidden and become a source of confusion in communicating ideas with others. Raul argued that using theories helped clarify understanding and therefore supported students to explain more effectively. Although Steven argued that the students talked more in Mrs. Glenda's room, Raul did not agree. Students' experiences may have differed across the classes. It was quite possible that Steven did participate more in talking about his ideas in Mrs. Glenda's class whereas Raul did not experience such a shift.

In the last interview, Raul and Steven also emphasized how terms and concepts like 'theory' helped them explain their ideas.

> *Raul:*   Another thing I liked, it helped me at least to talk, not to talk like I'm talking right now, it helps me explain things better because she taught us words and stuff, which I wouldn't know and I probably woulda used them wrong [inaudible].
>
> *Steven:* We woulda never known what a theory is [inaudible] but we know now.
>
> *Leslie:* Do you think your theories are important?
>
> *Raul:*   In the thing, yeah, our reasons like why. WHY. Why is like a very good question because I mean it's like an everyday question but like without why like there are a lot of things that people don't know. Like people might make a [inaudible] why or something. Like make something that they didn't even mean to and then they're like why? They start to try and figure out why and how it happened and then if the thing is usable they can like use it to do what they want.

Here Raul emphasized the importance of answering why and how questions. Without answers to these questions, he argued that there are many things that we would not know. Because the end of the unit focused on building, Raul's argument focused on the role that answering how and why questions could play in determining the utility of a rendered design. Throughout these interviews, Raul emphasized the primary role that the classroom played in helping him create more effective explanations of phenomena. Raul developed his capacity to explain more effectively over time while also strengthening his identification with key norms and values about the essential role of theory-building and explanation in science (Rutherford & Ahlgren, 1990). He also developed a capacity to talk about the role of his explanatory stance in his learning. His enthusiasm for explaining led him to talk over or talk for other students at particular points in time. His case illustrates what Holland et al. (1998) also found in their studies, that competence and identification co-evolve, that ways of knowing, doing, and being were integrated together in Raul's experience of learning science.

Facilitating Joint Understanding of Key Concepts and Ideas

Raul's focus on explanations could lead him to talk over his small-group members. However, his enthusiasm for explanation as a way of thinking and speaking about scientific ideas also helped him facilitate joint understanding in the classroom. Raul was regularly reminding other students' about the meaning of prediction and theory. He also evaluated whether or not what the reporters were presenting met the agreed upon definition of these terms.

On Day 3, Raul followed his peers' ideas and was able to evaluate whether or not they were providing theories for their group's work. Early in the reporting period he noticed that the reporters had not presented predictions or theories. He asked the question, "what do you think is gonna come down, and why do you think it's gonna come down, which side?," to prompt reporters to provide a prediction and a theory for the class. At the end of the reporting session, he was also quick to respond to Mrs. Glenda's questions about whether or not students were satisfied that predictions and theories were presented. Raul said, "yeah, I heard a prediction" or "I'm satisfied, yup" as Mrs. Glenda was seeking feedback about whether or not they could move to the next step in reporting. Raul's ability to ask successful questions and monitor his peers' responses showed that early in their work together he was developing an understanding of "theory." He understood what kinds of questions to ask to support other students to better communicate their ideas and develop shared meaning around new terms and concepts.

On Day 4, Raul prompted the class to have an explicit conversation about prediction and theory as terms and concepts that must have shared definitions. Rich had restated the theory that Raul's group presented. Raul objected to what Rich said. He argued that Rich had discussed how the theory worked but had not restated the theory itself. This pushed the class, with follow-through by Mrs. Glenda, into a discussion of what constitutes a prediction and a theory. The students expressed confusion about the definition of prediction and how it was similar or different from theory. As the confusion mounted, Mrs. Glenda responded directly to students who were saying things like, "the theory is like the results." Mrs. Glenda stopped the students and said, " I'm glad we got into here [this point of confusion]. Ok, you guys, ok the prediction is the I guess." She then began to state what a theory was when Raul stepped in to say the theory was the "why you think." Mrs. Glenda legitimized his point and reiterated to the class, "it's the why you think." Raul has pinpointed one of the fundamental scientific concepts in the class and was able to press for opportunities to create shared understanding of "theory" for the entire class.

On Day 5, the students revisited the definition of these key terms with Steven and Raul's assistance. Olivia and Rosie were reporting for their group when Steven asked for their theory remarking that he had not heard one presented. The girls said that they would present their theory in a minute. When they failed to do this again, Raul stepped in and asked for the theory again saying, "I didn't hear a theory." Qing claimed to hear a theory and Mrs. Glenda asked her to restate it for the class. Qing said, "I thought it will balance, that's what I heard, is that right?" Raul quickly jumped in and said, "That's the prediction. That's not the theory." Denise opted in at this point and said, "why they thought it would balance" would have met the criteria for theory-ness. Raul affirmed her statement. Together the students worked again to clarify predictions and theories. After this point in the study, it was relatively rare for students to confuse these two terms unless it was a misstatement that was quickly self-corrected. Over the first days of the study Raul led the charge in helping all students to share this important starting point for their work together – that theories answered the question "why" or "how" something happened.

Taking Perspectives/Negotiating Differences

Raul also brought an ability to take others' perspectives. This turned out to be a significant contribution to the classroom discussions. Raul often adjudicated debates and demonstrated how he understood someone's perspective.

During reporting on the baseline day, Denise and Olivia set up a problem and students tried to make their predictions. Confusion ensued as to which side was the left or the right of the balance scale because the students were sitting in a physical arrangement that did not allow for a shared line of sight to the scale. Students became frustrated and voices rose with cries of "this is the left!" or "that's the right!" Raul broke the confusion with a large gesture toward the scale and said, "you see it depends the way you're facing. If you're facing this way, this is your left. If you facing that way, this is your left." He explained that the left and right were relative to one's position to an object. Raul clarified this with a tone of frustration, as if to say, "why are we wasting time on this. Don't you get it!" After this comment he even showed aggravation with a quick shake of his head and an "urr." Mrs. Glenda followed up by saying that he had an excellent point and that the class needed to agree on what was the left and the right. Mrs. Glenda legitimized Raul's comment. After her comments, Raul's body shifted. He faced his classmates and rose higher up on his knees with his arms crossed in what might be seen as a more engaged and maybe even a more authoritative stance. His ability to take others' perspectives was clear from the baseline day.

On Day 5, after Denise presented her group's "double the distance to double the weight" theory, Rich challenged it. Raul, on the other hand said, "That looks pretty true" and together with Mrs. Glenda worked to test the theory using parallel problems that would double distances on one side of the balance scale and double weights on the other. Raul was quickly able to take up Denise's group's new theory in a way that allowed him to see the value in their perspective. He was also able to make the connection to the experience he and Steven had using the seesaw. He argued that although he weighed more than Steven they were able to balance because he moved toward the middle and Steven stayed at the end. Raul's ability to take perspectives was once again essential in the ongoing negotiation of central ideas in the classroom.

On Day 7, there was confusion and tension between Qing and Rich over predictions and results. Rich was challenging Qing's claim that the scale would not balance. Raul intervened to try and adjudicate the debate by saying, "the way they're placed it will not balance but it could balance if you would have placed it a different way." Raul was trying to take Rich's perspective and diffuse the tension that was mounting. Raul employed counterfactual reasoning that is vital to scientific thinking. Yet, Rich continued with his challenging. Mrs. Glenda interceded to tell everyone that the discussion had gotten too heated after Qing was clearly indicating that she was frustrated at being charged with presenting the problem incorrectly. Mrs. Glenda wanted to emphasize this point. Although Qing had presented the problem wrong she argued that "you should give that person a little bit more respect than you're giving them." As Mrs. Glenda continued to explicitly address the tension and "tune" (Haroutunian-Gordon & Waks, in press) herself to the students' uptake of new rules of engagement, Rich continued to aggravate the situation by not listening to what Mrs. Glenda was saying and arguing that Qing was also at fault. Qing reacted defensively. Raul interjected, "wait shush, you guys are getting angry at each other for no reason." Mrs. Glenda confirmed this, saying "right." Raul reemphasized with a frustrated tone, "just stop." At this point, Mrs. Glenda turned to address what she thought was motivating Rich's entrenchment, Qing's earlier claim that she did not predict but rather "knew" what was going to happen. Raul had tried to soften Qing's initial claim after Rich had challenged it by saying, "she's sayin' she thinks she knows . . . " Raul demonstrated maturity throughout this interaction. First he explicitly took up Rich's perspective in an effort to diffuse the debate with Qing. When Rich continued to be argumentative, Raul worked together with Mrs. Glenda to point out the need to listen to one another to move on with the work. As time went on in the study, Raul began to position himself as a person who understood and appreciated others' perspectives while also emphasizing that discussion of these perspectives must be fruitful and lead to further understanding.

On Day 9, Raul once again took up the role of mediator between the class and a particular student's ideas. He paraphrased what Rosie presented to the class when other students were vocal about not understanding what she said. Rosie talked about a hypothetical situation where media reporters came to look at her soda straw bridge (see Investigation #8, p. 38). With all the reporters crowding around the bridge and breathing and blowing on it during their careful inspections she wanted to know if the bridge would fall or stay up. Students expressed confusion about what she said. Mrs. Glenda said she understood Rosie and offered to paraphrase her ideas for the class. Raul jumped in and said that he also knew what Rosie was saying. He proceeded to re-voice Rosie's story.

> *Raul:* She's saying that if you had a straw bridge that you hafta make it really strong because she's saying that if there a lot of reporters and stuff and if they were looking at your bridge and if they were blowing then, she wants to know if the bridge would fall over or if it would stay up.

Raul stepped in to rearticulate the hypothetical context and question Rosie was trying to ask the class. At that moment, Mrs. Glenda looked up at Leslie with a smile, seemingly pleased and impressed with Raul's ability to follow and re-voice Rosie's ideas.

During the last interview after the study was completed, Raul explained that he liked how students could come up with their own ideas in Mrs. Glenda's class. He reported that this was different from his regular classroom science. He gave an example of what happened in his regular science classroom.

> *Raul:* Yesterday I was doing electricity and trying to make a light bulb light up [in my regular science class] and we were trying with graphite which is in a pencil and we were trying to see if electricity could travel through graphite and we didn't get it to light up at first. Then Mrs. Smith

> said we were doing it the wrong way and stuff. And I
> didn't exactly like that.

Leslie: What didn't you like about that?

Raul: We were trying to find our own way and trying to see
if certain things would work. But Mrs. Smith was saying
like you're doing it the wrong way and stuff. I was trying
to see if there were other ways to try and make the light
light up. Most of them didn't work but at least we tried
and then you might find out that there is another way.
And if you don't, then you'll just know one way.

Raul's comments help to explain his interest in taking others' perspectives. He valued the fact that students could and should come up
with their own ideas and that more alternatives were better than just
one. He had mentioned earlier in this interview that he appreciated
that Mrs. Glenda encouraged them to develop their own theories and
ideas to explain what they found out through their investigations. For
Raul, science was not a process of following directions to get correct
answers. It was a process of exploring ideas he did not necessarily
know to be "right" to find out something new. This required everyone in his class to listen to others' ideas and see how they worked,
perhaps in a new and unexpected way, to help further understanding
of a scientific question. This is a hallmark of becoming a scientist,
rising to the challenge of taking up problems to find new solutions,
and learning through tinkering, or what Kirsh and Maglio (1994) call
"epistemic actions." Combining this stance with Raul's appreciation
for the power of explanation in science and we see that for a fourth
grader he had developed surprisingly mature and complex ways of
knowing, doing, and being in science, so much so that he missed
their engagement in another science class where the teacher did not
bring this pedagogy to the classroom.

Raul stood out as an expressive leader who valued explanation in
science and negotiated differences and conflicting agendas among his
peers. He emerged as a sort of "diplomat" within class interactions. A
diplomat has an agenda yet learns to work successfully with others by
taking their perspectives. As his agenda, Raul took up the intellectual
norms and roles in the classroom to create and evaluate scientific

explanations while working to clarify and support other students to join him in this endeavor. Through his efforts he supported his own and other students' learning.

Christie

Christie was a European-American lower SES "neighborhood kid." She was not a strong student. Although she and her family agreed to her participation in the study, she was not an enthusiastic classroom member at first. She arrived for the first class session with a dour expression and bad attitude, refusing to participate, lying on the rug, and complaining. Mrs. Glenda knew a little about Christie because she had older siblings who had gone to the school. Mrs. Glenda reported that Christie was "my kinda kid." During daily reflections, Mrs. Glenda spontaneously talked about Christie more than any other student in the classroom. Although Christie was in the bottom three questioners in the classroom, she experienced one of the most dramatic personal transformations in the study. Over the course of the study, Christie went from assuming a defensive, resistant posture to a more confident, engaged approach.

After the baseline and Day 1 of the study when Mrs. Glenda had a chance to observe Christie working in her small group and her lack of participation during whole-class reporting she reflected on Christie's work and needs.

> *Mrs. Glenda:* I think Christie is going to need a lot [1 second pause] a lot of support, on many levels. I think she's gonna need support on the academics, the getting it out in writing cuz even if you look at her writing compared to everyone else's hers is bigger and much more impulsive and I mean just look at this [points to a sample of Christie's writing] in comparison to this [points to a sample of another student's writing]. Everyone else seems to be able to master the space, master keeping it on a line, and she's having difficulties even organizing her thoughts. And I think her defenses are because of

> that. I think all of the defensive posture we're get-
> ting here is not a kid who feels good about herself. I
> think she shuts down when she thinks she can't do
> it and my guess is she thinks she can't do anything.
> She can't write, she can't talk, she can't think.

Mrs. Glenda was working to put together the pieces of what she had observed. Christie's mood was sour, her participation reluctant, and her writing about her ideas much less developed than the other students. Mrs. Glenda believed that Christie was going to need significant support to make necessary academic changes and to build confidence in her abilities. At the same time, Mrs. Glenda did not shift expectations for Christie. Mrs. Glenda wanted Christie to be engaged in working together with her small group and successful at communicating her thinking in small-group and whole-class contexts. Mrs. Glenda and Leslie both noticed that Christie and Denise had tense interactions during small-group activity on the first two days of the study (Baseline and Day 1). Denise overshadowed Christie with her confidence and willingness to offer ideas for the group. Christie remained sullen and withdrawn during small-group work time. In her Day 1 reflections, when she noted that Christie was not working together with her small group, Mrs. Glenda said, "I want to know how acceptable her [Christie's] unproductivity is to her peers [in her small group]." There was a danger in this group of allowing stronger more confident students, like Denise, to take over for and further confirm Christie's self-evaluations of her abilities. Mrs. Glenda knew that this was brewing in Christie's group. Christie presented a complex set of issues for Mrs. Glenda who began to develop her plan for supporting Christie's ways of knowing, doing, and being in science.

Day 2 was an important early victory for Mrs. Glenda in her efforts to support Christie's learning. As the small-group activities were beginning Mrs. Glenda had a chance to talk with Christie about her attitude. Christie told Mrs. Glenda that she did not like to talk and report in front of the class. Christie also said that she was "not good at anything." Mrs. Glenda encouraged her and affirmed the importance of her ideas for the class. Mrs. Glenda paid attention and genuinely engaged with Christie in an effort to interrupt unproductive interaction patterns and the positioning by others in her group as "not capable." If left unchecked, these patterns of interaction could confirm Christie's lack of confidence in herself and her ideas. Christie remained engaged as her group prepared their report for the class. She sat at the back of the rug during reporting but was sitting up and attentive. Her audience role was checking the relationship between predictions, theories, and results. Mrs. Glenda prompted her to ask a question of the reporters. Although the question she asked was not an important content-focused one, Christie succeeded in paying attention and participating in the whole-class context. This was an important first step. As the day was drawing to a close, Mrs. Glenda asked for a volunteer to summarize all of what the reporters had said during that first day of reports using audience roles. Christie volunteered. She stood up, walked to the front of the room, and sat down at Mrs. Glenda's feet. With Mrs. Glenda's support, Christie began the process of summarizing for the class. Mrs. Glenda affirmed Christie's participation saying, "Christie can do it. Christie's not only showing me she's talking me through it. This is wonderful." Other students also participated in summarizing which helped surface the fact that students were not yet certain about what the reporters said. Christie's participation was a significant accomplishment as far as Mrs. Glenda was concerned. During her reflections that day she said,

> *Mrs. Glenda:* Surprises, Christie, watching her come down front to explain even after telling me she hates to talk and she hates school and she's not good at anything. To have her take a big chance and come right up front, that thrilled me, that was the high point of my day.

Mrs. Glenda knew that this was an important step for Christie. She had worked well that day with Denise after a rocky start to their relationship. She had fully engaged in an entire lesson, even volunteering to take on what Mrs. Glenda called the hardest job of the day – to summarize everything that had been discussed. Mrs. Glenda was not under any illusions however. Her experience with special education students who had self-evaluations similar to Christie's helped her realize just how challenging it would be to support Christie's engagement.

> *Mrs. Glenda:* I want Christie to see herself as a valuable person.... She's my kinda kid. She's a kid who does not have much and she's a kid who is very easily flustered. She's not the kind of kid in class who is ever gonna willingly show anybody that she's capable of contributing a whole lot in a positive way. If you can get it with a kid like that, if you can get a kid like Christie to sit and act like they're interested [2 second pause] it's just so challenging cuz [1 second pause] some of the kids are gonna do it whether or not you're there. They may not do exactly what you want but they're gonna be just fine. Christie is just a little hard.

Mrs. Glenda was well aware of the challenge she faced. Christie brought a history of negative self-evaluations. Christie also seemed to anticipate negative evaluations from her peers and her teacher. It was not going to be easy to set up a new set of experiences for Christie. Christie herself seemed to be a reluctant participant who was not going to "willingly show anybody that she's capable of contributing a whole lot in a positive way." She was protecting herself and needed constant, thoughtful intervention from Mrs. Glenda to take the risks associated with putting herself out there again. Mrs. Glenda knew that Christie needed opportunities to demonstrate to herself and others that "she could do it."

Disengagement, Disruption, and Negative Self-perception

Unfortunately, on Day 3 through the early part of reporting on Day 7, Christie was often disengaged, disinterested, and at times disruptive. Christie had a bad day on Day 3, having lost a tooth just before science with Mrs. Glenda. Christie had to go to the nurse's office for

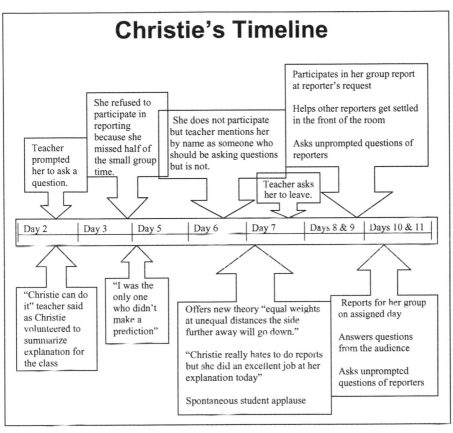

Figure 8. Christie's Timeline Across Instruction.

about half of the small-group work time and then didn't know what her group did. She was grumpy about this. This is understandable. For other students this might have been a minor setback, but for Christie, it felt like a major one because on this day she was assigned to be a reporter. [2] She did not want other students to ask her any questions about the work as a result of having not been there to participate. She and Carson stood at the front of the room, eyes facing the floor, not knowing how to begin. She did not say a word for the entire reporting session, even when she was an audience member.

---

[2] After Christie's experience Mrs. Glenda and Leslie tried as much as possible to support students who were not there to make choices about their participation during reporting sessions especially when they were supposed to act as reporters for their group.

When she was interviewed after Day 3, she said she did not like reporting.

> Leslie: Is there anything you don't like about science with Mrs. Glenda?
>
> Christie: To report.
>
> Leslie: You don't like to report, and why don't you like to report?
>
> Christie: Cuz I don't like talkin' that much and plus sometimes I don't understand some of the questions the kids ask.

Christie had some very good reasons to dislike the role of reporter. She did not like to talk and she did not understand the questions other students asked. To be placed in the position of having to do this when one did not actually do the work must have been an additional source of frustration for her. The events of Day 3 seemed to undermine the early victories on Day 2.

On Days 4 through the early reports of Day 7, Christie was largely silent, withdrawn, or off-task during whole-class time. On Day 4 she said nothing and did not appear engaged. On Day 5 she took a small speaking turn to clarify that she was the only person in her group who didn't make a prediction, a nod to difficulties in the small-group work time. On Day 6 she said nothing. However, Mrs. Glenda mentioned Christie and several other students by name on Day 6 when she pointed out that she was doing the work of asking questions when students in the audience should have been responsible for it.

On Day 7 frustrations seemed to bubble over for everyone in the classroom. Mrs. Glenda had worked with Christie and her group during small-group work time and she knew that Christie had some important ideas to share. It was a hot day inside the school, Denise did not feel well during small-group work time and left the classroom for some time, and the whole class seemed agitated. This was also the day that Denise told Mrs. Glenda that the students felt upset because not all groups had a chance to report. The students did not transition well to the reporting part of the lesson. They continued to talk and work as Mrs. Glenda repeatedly asked for their attention and even offered sanctions if they did not settle down ("we will stay here until we're done and you will miss your busses."). It was an unusually challenging beginning to reports. When the students did finally begin reporting, Christie continued to play with materials and ignored the reporters. Mrs. Glenda asked her to leave the room and she did. This was a low point for Christie, Mrs. Glenda, and the entire class. However, the tension offered an opportunity to address Christie's disengagement as well as the larger concerns about reporting that Denise brought to Mrs. Glenda's attention. At the end of this unusual reporting session when they had finished just one report, Mrs. Glenda "honored Denise's criticism" and said that the next day she would have the students come right in and report about the remaining activities. She ended the session saying, "It's been a rough day all around the school – I don't know why."

Engagement, Participation, and Confidence

When the students gathered together on the following day to hear the last two reports from Day 7, Christie's group reported last. Dai and Carson were due to present, but Carson was absent when the group did the activity the day before. Mrs. Glenda asked Dai if he wanted Christie to help him because she knew Christie had written down predictions, theories, results, and relationships among them during small-group work time. He agreed and Christie began presenting for her group on a day when she was not assigned to be a reporter. Mrs. Glenda positioned Christie to be successful and negotiated her airtime with Dai. Christie confidently presented using her laboratory notebook. She asked students for clarification if she did not understand what they were asking. Mrs. Glenda supported her throughout by spontaneously clarifying her report for the other students. Mrs. Glenda also supported Christie by reframing questions asked by the audience members. When the students and Mrs. Glenda determined that Christie's theory ("equal weights at unequal distances the side further away will go down") was not yet represented on their theory chart, they added it there. As the report and the day were drawing to a close, Mrs. Glenda made the following remark:

"Can I say something before you guys leave? Christie really hates to do reports, but I think she really did an excellent job at her explanation today." The students spontaneously started clapping (the only time this happened during the entire study) and agreed saying, "she did" and "yeah." The applause and praise from her classmates clearly made Christie smile and see that her peers valued her ideas. This episode indicated the important role that the students played in creating a powerful learning environment where an encouraging emotional climate was combined with challenging questions about important ideas. The students seemed to know what was at stake for Christie even though no one addressed this explicitly with them. This was a remarkable turn of events engineered, orchestrated, and scaffolded moment-by-moment by Mrs. Glenda. Mrs. Glenda was determined to reorient Christie to be a full participant in the community. After asking her to leave the day before, the stakes seemed much higher. She needed to create an opportunity for Christie to succeed.

In the interview after Day 8, Christie was asked the same questions about what she liked and did not like about doing science with Mrs. Glenda. This time she presented a different and surprising view of what she liked:

Leslie:	Can you tell me anything you like about doing science with Mrs. Glenda?
Christie:	Building things and drawing.
Leslie:	Building things and drawing.
Christie:	Reporting.
Leslie:	Reporting. So you like reporting? Do you like reporting now? This is new isn't it? Is this something that you're just [pause]
Christie:	Startin' to like.
Leslie:	Ye, yeah.
Christie:	Yeah.
Leslie:	You're just starting to like it huh?
Christie:	Yeah.

Leslie:	Well, that's really neat, that's really interesting. Can you tell me a little bit more about that? Why do you think you're starting to like it?
Christie:	Because I'm getting used to being in a science group.

Christie was starting to like reporting. That was a surprising revelation. Leslie was caught off guard and struggled to articulate her response. Christie stepped in to help her. No one could have predicted Christie's shift. Christie had a very successful experience reporting on Day 8 but Leslie and Mrs. Glenda were not under any illusions that just one experience would turn things around. So, this came as a complete surprise to the adults in the classroom. This shift marks the power of a pivotal experience of success within the context of a supportive classroom community. By this point in the research project, Christie knew Mrs. Glenda and was able to get a sense of the underlying emotional climate in the classroom. In the moment, Leslie and Mrs. Glenda underestimated the power of this experience for Christie. Having Christie's interview that day was helpful to understand her changing attitudes in response to classroom instruction.

After Day 8, Christie participated in reporting sessions every day. She willingly took her turn at reporting on Day 10 and also took a turn on Day 9 because Denise asked for Christie's help because she was not there when the group completed the activities. Christie also asked Mrs. Glenda questions to clarify how reporting was organized ("Does the [role] chart change every day?"), answered important content focused questions from the audience ("why did you put the straws like this?"), and asked content relevant questions ("where did you find your theory in your findings?") when she was in the audience. With the exception of her participation on Day 2, all of Christie's speaking turns took place in the second half of the study.

During the last interview after the science program was over, Christie had questions for Leslie as she interviewed her. She wanted to know "who had the idea to do this science unit?" Why did you make up this science unit?" and "Who was the one who made up the groups?" She had clearly become more interested in what was going on in science and much more comfortable asking probing questions of others. Her last question about the small-group assignments led Leslie to ask her what she thought of the groups.

Leslie: What did you think about the groups?

Christie: Kinda fun.

Leslie: Kinda fun? Did you like working in your group?

Christie: Not really.

Leslie: Not really? What didn't you like about working with your group?

Christie: Sometimes when you wanna work and people say they're using that thing when they didn't even pick it up yet.

Leslie: So sometimes it's hard to cooperate with your group members. Do you think your group did a pretty good job though overall or do you think you had more problems?

Christie: Half-n-half.

Leslie: So sometimes you weren't able to work through them and sometimes you were?

Christie: Yeah.

Leslie: Do you think that you did better at the beginning or toward the end of your time working together?

Christie: Better toward the end.

Leslie: Better toward the end. So that's interesting. Can you tell me why you think that happened?

Christie: Maybe because I wasn't used to being in a group so after we started to get used to each other in those groups we got better.

Christie's assessment of how the group worked showed the complexity that the adults had observed. The whole experience was challenging and sometimes Christie did not like it. As time went on and the students developed relationships, things improved. Christie began to participate more fully and completely in her small group and she found her voice in whole-class contexts. Her confidence seemed to increase as she regularly opted into conversations and did not hesitate to ask for clarification when she did not understand what someone else said. Christie's case was one of moving from a disengaged and defensive stance to more confidently building and sharing ideas with others. Her improvisations were highly scaffolded and supported by Mrs. Glenda. Christie offered the class an opportunity to recognize the value in everyone's ideas and enact that in the classroom. She also provided a chance to see just how challenging putting ideas out in the world can be for some students. The spontaneous clapping after Christie's report on Day 8 demonstrated a kind of empathy that might not have been possible to see if Christie had not been a student in this class.

Conclusion

Each of these cases presents a different view of how the "same" classroom was experienced for each student. In tracing the social and material opportunities through these intrapersonal cases, although the classroom experience was "the same" on the surface, digging deeper reveals how it was substantially different underneath. Each student came with his or her own ways of knowing, being, and doing and built on their personal foundations. They also created, along with their other classmates and Mrs. Glenda, opportunities for students in the classroom to experience, own and exercise new ways of being, knowing, and doing science together as a class. Our four focal students in particular provided opportunities for the classroom to take up challenges in a constructive manner, to help everyone to speak for themselves, to understand and elaborate explanations, and to empower students who may otherwise have been disengaged and defensive. Mrs. Glenda was a remarkably important player in all of this, like a conductor for an orchestra. As Mrs. Glenda was finding a way to draw out the best of all the students and combine these strengths into a coherent community, each student was learning new ways to be, to do, and to know while creating their community together. Landscape design professor Iain Robertson (personal communication) says that, "Good design makes places more like themselves than they were before." These case studies demonstrate how this enacted classroom experience, in the hands of a remarkable teacher, allowed these students opportunities to improvise and become the best versions of themselves as well. The students succeeded in Bruner's task of creating their own versions of a school science world.

Conclusion

... the conception of the school as a social center is born of our entire demo-
cratic movement. Everywhere we see signs of the growing recognition that
the community owes to each one of its members the fullest opportunity for
development. Everywhere we see the growing recognition that the community life is defective and distorted except as it does thus care for all its
constituent parts. This is no longer viewed as a matter of charity, but as a
matter of justice – nay, even of something higher and better than justice –
a necessary phase of developing and growing life.

John Dewey (1902) *The school as the social center* (p. 86)

In the course of the past four chapters we have introduced
our broad view of learning and provided an empirical exploration
of what it might look like to see school-based science learning from
our perspective. Our purpose was to build a theoretical argument and
methodological approach for studying science learning in a way that
would account for the cognitive, social, and emotional dimensions of
learning. The first chapter described the context of the study and the
design-based approach we originally employed to initially examine
students' scientific thinking alone. Empirical chapters demonstrate
how our new broad view of learning and methodological approach
was applied to the classroom where we had already documented
significant science learning, as defined in narrower terms as ways of
knowing and doing (Herrenkohl & Guerra, 1998). The current analysis reveals how much we missed by focusing exclusively on ways of
knowing and doing in past research. Broadening our view of learning
to encompass ways of being opened new perspectives on how students understand and use scientific thinking and come to see themselves as participants in the world of school science. Through this

191

process we are able to show how this classroom provided, in Dewey's words, "the fullest opportunity for development."

We investigated how students took up new ways of being, knowing, and doing through their balance and building investigations that required them to take more responsibility for the cognitive and social work, bringing new emotional demands into the classroom as well. We showed how students ways of being, knowing, and doing emerged at the community level through ongoing interpersonal interaction guided by explicit supports (i.e., intellectual tools and social roles designed to support students to take on the role of questioners in their investigations) and a thoughtful, reflective teacher who cared about students as people and served as expert guide and facilitator. We followed along as the students took up the practice of questioning one another about essential ideas in science. Through this process, we watched students develop questioning as a way of being, knowing, and doing together. We then examined what else happened as the students took up this new role as questioners within their classroom and found that they had new opportunities to negotiate speaking rights, persist in the face of difficulty to understand and articulate ideas, take perspectives to support the exchange and understanding of ideas, challenge ideas, and demonstrate the important role that "being wrong" can play in science learning. Opportunities to engage Dewey's (1933) attitudes for inquiry, open-mindedness, whole-heartedness, and responsibility transformed students' classroom interactions in a way that revealed critical scientific thinking, spontaneous empathy and adjustments to other students' emotional states, and an ability to act with these aspects in mind.

We also presented four student case studies that demonstrated that each student had a unique personal trajectory inside their common classroom experience. Thinking scientifically was woven together with personal and collective interests, intentions, emotional commitments, and beliefs about how to be a person in science in the course of ongoing classroom lessons. Our goal has been to build a case for a robust account of learning that can more fully live up to Dewey's notion of the school as a social center, a place where we see students actively learn about the social as well as the intellectual meaning of the work in which they are engaged. Students developed wider understanding of science, themselves, their peers, and their social world.

While we embrace many of Dewey's big ideas, we are also eager to avoid the sentimentalism that Bruner (1962) in his essay "After John Dewey, What?" argues has haunted Dewey's legacy. One might disagree with Bruner's interpretation of Dewey, yet one cannot deny that Dewey's ideas are often viewed as idealistic. We want to explicitly address this issue of idealism in the face of our work and in connection to our use of Dewey's ideas. Our study may be unique, but we do not believe that it is idealistic or sentimental in any way. Bruner (1962) writes,

> It is sentimentalism to assume that the teaching of life can be fitted always to the child's interests just as it is empty formalism to force the child to parrot the formulas of adult society. Interest can be created and stimulated. In this sphere it is not far from the truth to say that supply creates demand, that the provocation of what is available creates response. One seeks to equip the child with deeper, more gripping, and subtler ways of knowing the world and himself. (pp. 117–118)

Our work demonstrates Bruner's claim that interest can be stimulated within activities that provoke students to deeply engage with the teacher, with each other, and with ideas that, on the surface, may seem to have relatively little connection to what might occupy students outside of school. Studying balance and building and developing an understanding of the multiplicative rule of torque is not likely to be every fourth grader's favorite hobby or free-time activity. However, it became inherently interesting to these students, so that they wanted more time to ask questions and to talk about their ideas. Mrs. Glenda and the students created a learning environment that privileged both powerful scientific thinking practices and the people engaging in those practices. We provided evidence of how students came to understand science and themselves as science learners in new ways a result of their participation. Examining how students emerged as people in the classroom setting allowed us to identify another kind of learning that all students must engage as they navigate their way through school. This was not a program to promote self-esteem. However, for some students, their confidence in themselves as people and thinkers substantially improved. This improvement was linked to building mastery and expertise as scientific thinkers, to students seeing themselves as valued participants in the complex and collaborative scientific thinking that came to characterize the classroom. With expert guidance and support from Mrs. Glenda, less-confident students like Christie worked hard to gain greater confidence and mastery and could see in their hard work a person they might not have seen very often in the past thus encouraging their further engagement. Students' new ways of knowing and doing developed together with new ways of being to propel the whole student forward as a thinker and a person.

The National Research Council (National Research Council, 2007; 2009) recently published two volumes on science learning. One addresses school-based learning (National Research Council, 2007) through focusing on four strands: scientific content; methods of investigation; meta-reflection on scientific thinking, processes, and practices; and socialization into scientific practice. The informal science learning volume (National Research Council, 2009) published after the school-based volume added two strands to the original four. The committee argued that there is a need to examine interest and motivation as well as engagement and identity if we are to fully understand scientific learning and understanding in out-of-school contexts. Our work provides an example of how one could take these two additional strands and make sense of how they are active and alive in school-based contexts as well. The emphasis in the first volume on school-based learning reveals a priority on ways of knowing and socially doing science together in these settings. Becoming a person who studies science was not the focus of the same amount of attention in the school-based volume. Our book makes the argument that these issues of being and becoming are not checked at the science classroom door. We must begin to conceptualize how students begin to see or not see themselves inside of school science practices in order to provide a complete picture of science learning (or not learning as the case may be). If we are to fully understand how people become scientifically literate citizens and choose scientific careers, we must revisit school-based discussions of learning so that they include interest, motivation, engagement, and identity.

Our book represents one step toward this important and ongoing challenge for the field. This book is a demonstration project, an existence proof that taking the broad view of learning we postulate here in theoretical and methodological terms adds to our understanding and answers questions that, to this point, have not been sufficiently addressed. Our specific findings from the classroom discourse analyses as well as student case studies would not necessarily be found in other classroom settings, yet the tools we use are equally applicable to all settings where we wish to examine the ways of knowing, doing, and being that are privileged in that setting. A widespread examination of learning from this broad view could inform the way we think about formal schooling and the opportunities to learn that are present and/or missing. These kinds of analyses would help us conceptualize civic participation in science and science career choice, two areas we believe require a broad view of learning to fully understand. Furthermore, there is a need to build a unified theory of science learning that can account for learning across time and contexts, both formal and informal. A broad view of learning in the future must consider science learning across much longer timescales (see Lemke, 2000) and across school, home, and community contexts (Bell, Bricker, Lee, Reeve, & Zimmerman, 2006; Bell, Zimmerman, Bricker, & Lee, 2006) that embrace different cultural practices relevant to developing ways of knowing, doing, and being in science (Nasir, Rosebery, & Warren, & Lee, 2006).

There are many implications that taking a broad view of learning can have on future work in the field. We will discuss four pressing areas where a broad view of learning could impact the ways we conceptualize and practice education.

Educational contexts can stigmatize students because they do not fit into the mainstream classroom culture (Anzaldua, 1987; Gonzalez, Moll, & Amanti, 2005; Heath, 1986; Lee, 2000). To address this stigmatization, we need to value the varied contributions students make in a socially and emotionally supportive and intellectually rigorous classroom environment. Although larger social categories such as race, sex, ethnicity, socioeconomic status, and language are important to understand in order to examine the wider social, political, and cultural context of schooling, we need to move beyond these categories alone to fully appreciate and recruit the repertoires students bring to the classroom (Heath, 1995; Gutierrez & Rogoff, 2003; Nasir, Rosebery, Warren, & Lee, 2006). All students bring strengths to the classroom but as teachers we may not be very adept at assessing and identifying these strengths and using them to benefit the entire class. Mrs. Glenda is a model for how to do this with students. With her expert intervention and guidance, Rich's challenges became an opportunity for social-emotional and academic learning for all students in the classroom. In some classroom contexts, a student like Rich would have spent more time being excluded from activities than being included, yet as we demonstrated, his presence was absolutely critical for key aspects of the classroom learning. Mrs. Glenda recognized Rich's intuitive thinking and his need for more practice in expressing his ideas. She embraced the opportunities he opened up in the classroom when he challenged others, although it is clear that at times it was not easy for her or the other students. Denise was another interesting case. A capable and thoughtful student who readily admitted being wrong and changing her mind, at first she tried to take over speaking turns for other students, positioning them as less competent as a result. Mrs. Glenda did not allow her to do this. Over time, Denise moved from trying to take over and speak for students to offering students opportunities to speak for themselves while maintaining her own strong voice in the classroom. Rich and Denise's repertoires of practice were a product of their cultural, historical, and personal experiences. However, social category labels do not reveal these repertoires. It was necessary to dig deeper and understand the consistent patterns of participation that marked important ways of being, knowing, and doing that each students brought to the classroom. When teachers do this, they can then encourage students to use and transform their repertoires to support their own and others' learning. In the case of Rich and Denise, their strengths could have easily been profound weaknesses that undermined their own and others' learning. The teacher's role in positioning and negotiating students' repertoires throughout the classroom lessons transformed them into strengths that positively affected the intellectual, social, and emotional learning. This suggests that to fully embrace learning from our broad view, we need to assess and recruit students' repertoires as strengths in the classroom.

A broad view of learning might also help effectively address the needs of students who underachieve, engage minimally in the experience of school, or drop out (e.g., Fine, 1991). Outside of school, students who are viewed as apathetic in school often independently create their own environments, activities, and pathways for learning (Barron, 2004; Bransford et al., 2006; Rogoff, 2003). Some students who are able to engage in an activity for extended periods of time in out-of-school contexts, report that their interest and desire to learn diminishes when they are in school (Mertl, 2009). These students do not recognize school's potential to help them reach future goals (Becker & Carper, 1956; Stevens, O'Connor, & Garrison, 2005; Wahl & Blackhurst, 2000). In addition, students may be seeking more autonomy than a traditional classroom affords. When we define learning solely as a knowledge-based activity and allow students ways of being to remain untapped, it can make it easier for students to decide that they don't care about a particular topic and disengage. However, when we conceptualize learning from a broad view, students' ways of being, their interests, skills, knowledge, abilities, and intentions all become an explicit part of what it means to learn in the classroom. These ways of being can be recruited regardless of content and provide the "provocation" in Bruner's words, for students to want to engage. In so doing, classrooms where a broad view of learning is reflectively embraced may make it less likely that students will disengage, even when the content is less interesting to them. We saw that in the students discussed in this book. All of them, including Christie, Emma, and Carson, the students who asked the fewest questions, engaged more significantly over time in the classroom even though the content was unlikely to be a favorite topic or subject for them. Academic achievement is positively correlated with a level of belongingness – whether manifest with peers, friends, the classroom climate, or through student-teacher relations (Baumeister & Leary, 1995). Students want to feel that they receive emotional and social support. Our broad view of learning provides a way to tether belongingness to the learning of important knowledge and skills. This has implications not only for school learning but also out-of-school and future career contexts where the ability to collaborate and engage other people for help and advice in distributed efforts in everyday, real-world settings is necessary (Mertl et al., 2008). The work of economist James Heckman and his colleagues (Heckman, Stixrud, & Krzua, 2006) demonstrates that locus of control, persistence, and self-esteem are as important to long-term economic success as academic achievement. As educators, we are challenged to have a more complex understanding of students' backgrounds and to build nurturing and demanding relationships to support students emotionally, intellectually, and socially by talking about how learning involves ways of being, knowing, and doing together.

Our perspective also has implications for instructional practices and teacher learning and development. If we conceptualize student learning as including ways of being, knowing, and doing, we must also begin to think about teacher learning within this same human science framework. In a recent review of literature on teacher social and emotional competence in relation to student and classroom outcomes, Jennings and Greenberg (2009) demonstrate that teachers' own well-being, as well as teacher-student relationships, is associated with student outcomes. Their review suggests that teachers who participated in programs that supported their own social-emotional awareness may be more effective at establishing supportive social and emotional learning communities in their classrooms. As a field, we need to know how teachers' opportunities for learning and professional development support them to create effective learning communities that engage students as thinkers and people. How can we think about social emotional awareness together with high leverage content-based teaching practices that are now being investigated in math and science instruction (Herrenkohl, White, & Tasker, under review; Franke, Kazemi, & Battey, 2007; Kazemi & Hubbard, 2008, and Lampert & Graziani, 2009; Windschitl, Thompson, & Braaten, 2008)? Although this book does not focus solely or exclusively on teacher learning and pedagogical practices, the instructional materials together with the teacher's actions and ongoing social, emotional, and academic assessments of students are highlighted as making important contributions to students' opportunities to learn.

Further work dedicated to understanding how teachers' social and emotional awareness as a domain-general construct comes together with domain-specific instructional practices would support our efforts to provide more effective professional development and pre-service teacher preparation based on our broad view of learning.

Finally, a broad view of learning is consistent with the burgeoning field investigating the connection between children's experiences and their developing brains (NRC, 2000). Recent reports of the success of the preschool program, Tools of the Mind (Bodrova & Leong, 1996), in developing young children's executive functioning such as the ability to focus attention and ignore distractions, retain and use information, plan and revise actions and ideas, and control impulses linked educational programming to neuroscience outcomes (Diamond, Barnett, Thomas, & Munro, 2007). Our work provides detailed analyses of how students developed sophisticated practices such as negotiating speaking rights, persisting in the face of difficulty to understand ideas, and revising thinking over time based on evidence. Better understanding ways of being and domain general abilities associated with executive functioning and how they connect (or not) to instructional approaches that engage students in the learning of important disciplinary content will be an important next step for neuroscientists, developmental psychologists, and educators. Ultimately, as Dewey argued over 100 years ago, "the community owes to each one of its members the fullest opportunity for development" (1902, p. 86).

References

Alsop, S. (2005). *Beyond Cartesian dualism. Encountering affect in the teaching and learning of science*. Dordrecht, The Netherlands: Springer.

Anzaldua, G. C. (1987). *Borderlands/La Frontiera: The new mestiza*. San Francisco: Spinster/Aunt Lute.

Bakhurst, D. (2007). Vygotsky's demons. In H. Daniels, M. Cole, & J. V. Wertsch (Eds.), *The Cambridge companion to Vygotsky* (pp. 50–76). Cambridge: Cambridge University Press.

Barron, B. (2003). When smart groups fail. *The Journal of the Learning Sciences*, 12(3), 307–359.

Barron, B. (2004). Learning ecologies for technological fluency: Gender and experience differences. *Journal of Educational Computing Research*, 31, 1–36.

Bateson, M. C. (1990). *Composing a life*. New York, NY: Penguin.

Baumeister, R. F., & Leary, M. R. (1995). The need to belong: Desire for interpersonal attachments as a fundamental human motivation. *Psychological Bulletin*, 117, 497–529.

Bearison, D. J. (1991). Interactional contexts of cognitive development: Piagetian approaches to sociogenesis. In L. T. Landsmann (Ed.), *Culture, cognition and schooling* (pp. 56–70). Norwood, NJ: Ablex.

Becker, H. S., & Carper, J. W. (1956). The development of identification with an occupation. *The American Journal of Sociology*, 61(4), 289–298.

Becker, H. (1982). School is a lousy place to learn anything in. *American Behavioral Scientist*, 16, 85–105.

Bell, P., Bricker, L. A., Lee, T. R., Reeve, S., & Zimmerman, H. T. (2006). Understanding the cultural foundations of children's biological knowledge: Insights from everyday cognition research. In S. A. Barab, K. E. Hay, & D. T. Hickey (Eds.), *Proceedings from the Seventh International Conference of the Learning Sciences* (pp. 1029–1035). Mahwah, NJ: Lawrence Erlbaum.

Bell, P., Zimmerman, H. T., Bricker, L. A., & Lee, T. (2006). *The everyday cultural foundations of children's biological understanding in an urban, high-poverty community*. Paper presented at the National Association for Research in Science Teaching (NARST), San Francisco, CA.

Bodrova, E., & Leong, D. J. (1996). *Tools of the mind: The Vygotskian approach to early childhood education*. Englewood Cliffs, NJ: Merrill/Prentice Hall.

Bourdieu, P. (1977). *Outline of a theory of practice* (R. Nice, Trans.). Cambridge, UK: Cambridge University Press.

Bransford, J., Vye, N., Stevens, R., Kuhl, P., Schwartz, D., Bell, P., et al. (2006). Learning theories and education: Toward a decade of synergy. In P. Alexander & P. Winne (Eds.), *Handbook of education psychology*. Mahwah, NJ: Lawrence Erlbaum.

Brown, A. L. (1992). Design experiments: Theoretical and methodological challenges in creating complex interventions in classroom settings. *Journal of the Learning Sciences, 2*, 141–178.

Brown, A. L. (1997). Transforming schools into communities of thinking and learning about serious matters. *American Psychologist, 52(4)*, 399–413.

Brown, A. L., & Campione, J. C. (1990). Communities of learning and thinking, or a context by any other name. In D. Kuhn (Ed.), *Developmental perspectives on teaching and learning thinking skills*. New York, NY: Kanger.

Brown, A. L., & Campione, J. C. (1994). Guided discovery in a community of learners. In K. McGilly (Ed.), *Classroom lessons: Integrating cognitive theory and classroom practice* (pp. 229–270). Cambridge, MA: MIT Press.

Brown, A. L., & Campione, J. C. (1996). Psychological theory and the design of innovative learning environments: On procedures, principles, and systems. In L. Schauble & R. Glaser (Eds.), *Innovation in learning: New environments for education* (pp. 289–325). Mahwah, NJ: Lawrence Erlbaum.

Bruer, J. T. (1993). *Schools for thought: A science of learning in the classroom*. Cambridge, MA: MIT Press.

Bruner, J. (1962). *On knowing: Essays for the left hand*. Cambridge, Mass.: The Belknap Press of Harvard University Press.

Burke, K. (1945). *Grammar of motives*. New York, NY: Prentice Hall.

Butterfield, E. C., & Nelson, G. D. (1991). Promoting positive transfer of different types. *Cognition and Instruction, 8*, 69–102.

Carey, S., & Smith, C. (1993). On understanding the nature of scientific knowledge. *Educational Psychologist, 28*, 235–251.

Cazden, C. B. (1988). *Classroom discourse: The language of teaching and learning*. Portsmouth, NH: Heinemann.

Chapin, S. H., O'Connor, C., & Anderson, N. C. (2009). *Classroom discussions: Using math talk to help students learn*. Sausalito, CA: Math Solutions.

Chinn, C. A., & Brewer, W. F. (1993). The role of anomalous data in knowledge acquisition: A theoretical framework and implications for scienceinstruction. *Review of Educational Research, 63*, 1–49.

Cobb, P., & Yackel, E. (1996). Constructivist, emergent, and sociocultural perspectives in the context of developmental research. *Educational Psychologist, 31*, 175–190.

Cohen, E. G. (1984). Talking and working together: Status, interaction and learning. In P. Peterson, L. C. Wilkinson & M. Hallinan (Eds.), *The social context of instruction: Group organization and group process* (pp. 171–189). New York, NY: Academic.

Cohen, E. G. (1990). Teaching in multiculturally heterogeneous classrooms: Findings from a model program. *McGill Journal of Education, 26(1)*, 7–23.

Cohen, E. G. (1994). *Designing groupwork: Strategies for the heterogeneous classroom* (2 ed.). New York, NY: Teachers College Press.

Cole, M. (1996). *Cultural psychology: A once and future discipline*. Cambridge, MA: Harvard University Press.

Cornelius, L., & Herrenkohl, L. R. (2004). Power in the classroom: How the classroom environment shapes students' relationships with each other and with concepts. *Cognition and Instruction*, 22(4), 467–498.

Cubberley, E. P. (1919). *Public education in the United States: A study and interpretation of American educational history.* New York, NY: Houghton Mifflin.

Damon, W. (1983). *Social and personality development: Infancy through adolescence.* New York, NY: W.W. Norton.

Daniels, H., Cole, M., & Wertsch, J. V. (Eds.). (2007). *The Cambridge companion to Vygotsky.* Cambridge: Cambridge University Press.

DeAvila, E. A. (1987). *Finding out/descubrimiento.* Northvale, NJ: Santillana.

Dewey, J. (1902). The school as the socialcenter. *The Elementary School Teacher*, 3(2), 73–86.

Dewey, J. (1916). *Democracy and education.* New York, NY: The Free Press.

Dewey, J. (1933). *How we think.* Boston: D.C. Heath & Company.

Diamond, A., Barnett, W. S., Thomas, J., & Munro, S. (2007). Preschool program improves cognitive control. *Science*, 318(5855), 1387–1388.

Dreeban, R. (1968). *On what is learned in school.* Reading, MA: Addison-Wesley.

Dreyfus, H. L. (1984). What expert systems can't do. *Raritan*, 3(4), 22–36.

Driver, R., Asoko, H., Leach, J., Mortimer, E., & Scott, P. (1994). Constructing scientific knowledge in the classroom. *Educational Researcher*, 23, 5–12.

Dyson, A. H. (1995). The courage to write: Child meaning making in a contested world. *Language Arts*, 72(5), 324–333.

Edwards, D., & Mercer, N. (1987). *Common knowledge: The development of understanding in the classroom.* London: Methuen.

Engle, R. A., & Conant, F. C. (2002). Guiding principles for fostering productive disciplinary engagement: Explaining an emergent argument in a community of learners classroom. *Cognition and Instruction*, 20(4399–483).

Engle, R. A., McKinney de Royston, M., & Langer-Osuna, J. (2008). *Toward a model of differential influence in discussions: Negotiating quality, authority, and access within a heated classroom argument.* Paper presented at the Cognitive Science Society, Washington, DC.

Erickson, F. (2002). Culture and human development. *Human Development*, 15(4), 299–306.

Erickson, F. (2006). Definition and analysis of data from videotape: Some research procedures and their rationales. In J. L. Green, G. Camilli, & P. Elmore (Eds.), *Handbook of complementary methods in education research* (pp. 177–191). Mahwah, NJ: Lawrence Erlbaum.

Erikson, E. H. (1950). *Childhood and society.* New York, NY: W.W. Norton & Company, Inc.

Erikson, E. H. (1968). *Identity, youth, and crisis.* New York, NY: W.W. Norton & Company, Inc.

Esmonde, I., & Langer-Osuna, J. (2007). *Power in numbers: An analysis of how shifts in social and mathematical power among students in a cooperative group affect opportunities for learning.* Paper presented at the American Educational Research Association, Chicago, IL.

Fine, M. (1991). *Framing dropouts.* Albany, NY: State University of New York Press.

Flanders, N. A. (1970). *Analysing teaching behaviour.* Reading, MA: Addison-Wesley.

Flyvbjerg, B. (2001). *Making social science matter: Why social inquiry fails and how it can succeed again.* New York, NY: Cambridge University Press.

Forman, E. A., & Ansell, E. (2002). Orchestrating the multiple voices and inscriptions of a mathematics classroom. *The Journal of the Learning Sciences,* 11*(2&3),* 251–274.

Forman, E. A., & Ansell, E. (2005). Creating mathematics stories: Learning to explain in a third-grade classroom. In R. Nemirovsky, A. S. Rosebery, J. Solomon & B. Warren (Eds.), *Everyday matters in science and mathematics: Studies of complex classroom events.* Mahwah, NJ: Lawrence Erlbaum.

Foucault, M. (1999). Power as knowledge. In C. Lemert (Ed.), *Social theory: The multicultural and classic readings* (pp. 475–478). Boulder, CO: Westview.

Franke, M. L., Kazemi, E., & Battey, D. (2007). Mathematics teaching and classroom practice. In J. F. K. Lester (Ed.), *Second handbook of research on mathematics teaching and learning* (pp. 225–256). Charlotte, NC: Information Age Publishing.

Gee, J. (1990). *Social linguistics and literacies: Ideology in discourses.* London, UK: Falmer Press.

Gergen, K. (1991). *The saturated self: Dilemmas of identity in contemporary life.* New York, NY: Basic Books.

Goffman, E. (1959). *The presentation of self in everyday life.* Garden City, NJ: Doubleday.

Gonzalez, N., Moll, L. C., & Amanti, C. (2005). *Funds of knowledge: Theorizing practices in households, communities, and classrooms.* Mahwah, NJ: Lawrence Erlbaum.

Goodnow, J. J. (1990). The socialization of cognition: What's involved? In J. W. Stigler, R. A. Shweder & G. Herdt (Eds.), *Cultural psychology: Essays on comparative human development* (pp. 259–286). New York, NY: Cambridge University Press.

Graff, G. (1992). *Beyond the culture wars: How teaching the conflicts can revitalize American education.* New York, NY: W.W. Norton & Company, Inc.

Graves, D. (1983). *Writing: Teachers and Children at work.* Portsmouth, NH: Heinemann.

Greenberg, M. T., Weissberg, R. P., O'Brien, M. U., Zins, J. E., Fredericks, L., Resnik, H., et al. (2003). Enhancing school-based prevention and youth development through coordinated social, emotional, and academic learning. *American Psychologist,* 58*(6–7),* 466–474.

Greeno, J. G. (1997). On claims that answer the wrong questions. *Educational Researcher,* 26*(1),* 5–17.

Greeno, J. G. (1998). The situativity of knowing, learning, and research. *American Psychologist,* 53*(1),* 5–26.

Greeno, J. G. (2002). *Students with competence, authority, and accountability: Affording intellective identities in classrooms.* New York, NY: The College Board.

Gresalfi, M. S. (2009). Taking up opportunities to learn: Constructing dispositions in mathematics classrooms. *Journal of the Learning Sciences,* 18*(3),* 327–369.

Gutiérrez, K., & Stone, L. (2000). Synchronic and diachronic dimensions of social practice: An emerging methodology for cultural-historical perspectives on literacy learning. In C. D. Lee & P. Smagorinsky (Eds.), *Vygotskian perspectives on literacy research: Constructing meaning through collaborative inquiry* (pp. 150–164). Cambridge, UK: Cambridge University Press.

Gutierrez, K. D., & Rogoff, B. (2003). Cultural ways of learning: Individual traits or repertoires of practice. *Educational Researcher*, 22(5), 19–25.

Haroutunian-Gordon, S., & Waks, L. J. (in press). Listening: Challenges for teachers. *Teachers College Record*.

Harter, S. (1999). *The construction of self: A developmental perspective*. New York, NY: Guilford Press.

Heath, S. B. (1986). Sociocultural contexts of language development. In *Beyond Language: Social and Cultural Factors in Schooling Language Minority Students*. Los Angeles, CA: Evaluation, Dissemination, and Assessment Center.

Heath, S. B. (1995). Race, ethnicity, and the defiance of categories. In W. D. Hawley & A. W. Jackson (Eds.), *Toward A Common Destiny: Improving Race And Ethnic Relations in America* (pp. 39–70). San Francisco, CA: Jossey-Bass.

Heckman, J. J., Stixrud, J., & Urzua, S. (2006). The effects of cognitive and noncognitive abilities on labor market outcomes and social behaviors. *Journal of Labor Economics*, 24(3), 411–482.

Hegedus, S. J., & Penuel, W. R. (2008). Studying new forms of participation and identity in mathematics classrooms with integrated communication and representational infrastructures. *Educational Studies in Mathematics*, 68(2), 171–183.

Herrenkohl, L. R., & Guerra, M. R. (1998). Participation structure, scientific discourse, and student engagement in fourth grade. *Cognition and Instruction*, 16(4), 431–473.

Herrenkohl, L. R., & Guerra, M. R. (1999). Moving classrooms beyond transmission models of teaching and learning. In R. Bibace, J. J. Dillon & B. N. Dowds (Eds.), *Partnerships in research, clinical and educational settings* (Vol. 18, pp. 161–178). Stamford, CT: Ablex.

Herrenkohl, L. R., Palinscar, A. S., DeWater, L. S., & Kawasaki, K. (1999). Developing scientific communities in classrooms: A sociocognitive approach. *The Journal of the Learning Sciences*, 8(3 & 4), 451–493.

Herrenkohl, L. R., & Wertsch, J. V. (1999). The use of cultural tools: Mastery and appropriation. In I. Sigel (Ed.), *Development of mental representation: Theories and applications* (pp. 415–435). Mahwah, NJ: Lawrence Erlbaum.

Herrenkohl, L.R., White, B., Tasker, T. (under review). Pedagogical practices to support classroom cultures of scientific inquiry.

Hickey, D. T., & Schafer, N. J. (2006). Sociocultural, knowledge-centered views of classroom management. In C. Evertson & C. Weinstein (Eds.), *Handbook of classroom management: Research, practice, & contemporary issues* (pp. 281–308). New York, NY: Simon & Schuster Macmillan.

Hicks, D. (1996). *Discourse, learning, and schooling*. New York, NY: Cambridge University Press.

Hinde, R. A., Perret-Clermont, A. N., & Stevenson-Hinde, J. (Eds.). (1985). *Social relationships and cognitive development*. Oxford: Clarendon Press.

Holland, D., & Lachicotte, W. (2007). Vygotsky, Mead, and the new sociocultural studies of identity. In H. Daniels, M. Cole, & J. V. Wertsch (Eds.), *The Cambridge companion to Vygotsky* (pp. 101–135). New York, NY: Cambridge University Press.

Holland, D., Lachicotte, W., Skinner, D., & Cain, C. (1998). *Identity and agency in cultural worlds*. Cambridge, MA: Harvard University Press.

Jennings, P. A., & Greenberg, M. T. (2009). The prosocial classroom: Teacher social and emotional competence in relation to student and classroom outcomes. *Review of Educational Research, 79(1)*, 491–525.

John-Steiner, V. (2000). *Creative collaboration*. New York, NY: Oxford University Press.

Karmiloff-Smith, A., & Inhelder, B. (1974). If you want to get ahead, get a theory. *Cognition, 3(3)*, 195–212.

Kawasaki, K., Herrenkohl, L. R., & Yeary, S. A. (2004). Theory building and modeling in a sinking and floating unit: A case study of third and fourth grade students' developing epistemologies of science. *International Journal of Science Education, 26(11)*, 1299–1324.

Kazemi, E., & Hubbard, A. (2008). New directions for the design and study of professional development: Attending to the coevolution of teachers' participation across contexts. *Journal of Teacher Education, 59(5)*, 428–441.

Kirsh, D., & Maglio, P. (1994). On distinguishing epistemic from pragmatic action. *Cognitive Science, 18*, 513–549.

Kuhn, D. (1992). Thinking as argument. *Harvard Educational Review, 62*, 155–78.

Kuhn, D. (1993). Science as argument: Implications for teaching and learning scientific thinking. *Science Education, 77*, 319–337.

Lampert, M. (1990). When the problem is not the question and the solution is not the answer: Mathematical knowing and teaching. *American Educational Research Journal, 27(1)*, 29–63.

Lampert, M., & Graziani, F. (2009). Instructional activities as a tool for teachers' and teacher educators' learning. *Elementary School Journal, 109(5)*, 491–509.

Lave, J. (1988). *Cognition in practice*. Cambridge, UK: Cambridge University Press.

Lave, J., & Wenger, E. (1991). *Situated learning: Legitimate peripheral participation*. Cambridge, UK: Cambridge University Press.

Lee, C. D. (1995). A culturally based cognitive apprenticeship: Teaching African American high school students' skill in literacy interpretation. *Reading Research Quarterly, 30*, 608–630.

Lee, C. D. (2000). Signifying in the zone of proximal development. In C. D. Lee & P. Smagorinsky (Eds.), *Vygotskian Perspectives on Literacy Research: Constructing meaning through collaborative inquiry* (pp. 191–225). Cambridge, UK: Cambridge University Press.

Lee, C. D. (2001). Is October Brown Chinese? A cultural modeling activity system for underachieving students. *American Educational Research Journal, 38*, 97–141.

Lehrer, R., & Schauble, L. (2005). Developing modeling and argument in the elementary grades. In T. A. Romberg, T. P. Carpenter & F. Dremock (Eds.), *Understanding mathematics and science matters* (pp. 29–53). Mahwah, NJ: Lawrence Erlbaum.

Lemke, J. (2000). The long and the short of it: Comments on multiple timescale studies of human activity. *Journal of the Learning Sciences, 10(1–2)*, 193–202.

Lemke, J. (2000). Across the scales of time: artifacts, activities, and meanings in ecosocial systems. *Mind, Culture, and Activity, 7(4)*, 273–290.

Lemke, J. L. (1990). *Talking science: Language, learning, and values*. Norwood, NJ: Ablex Publishing Corporation.

Lewis, C., Perry, R., & Murata, A. (2006). How should research contribute to instructional improvement? The case of lesson study. *Educational Researcher*, 35(3), 3–14.

Marcia, J. E. (1980). Identity in adolescence. In J. Adelson (Ed.), *Handbook of adolescent psychology* (pp. 159–187). New York, NY: John Wiley and Sons.

Matthews, G. B. (1980). *Philosophy and the young child.* Cambridge, MA: Harvard University Press.

Matthews, G. B. (1984). *The philosophy of childhood.* Cambridge, MA: Harvard University Press.

Matthews, W. (1984). Influences on the learning and participation of minorities in mathematics. *Journal for Research in Mathematics Education*, 15(2), 84–95.

Matusov, E. (1996). Intersubjectivity without agreement. *Mind, Culture and Activity*, 3, 25–45.

Mehan, H. (1979). *Learning lessons: Social organization in the classroom.* Cambridge, MA: Harvard University Press.

Mercier, E., Mertl, V., Tyson, K., Barron, B., Herrenkohl, L., Nasir, N., et al. (2008). *Repertoires of collaborative practice: A theoretical introduction.* Paper presented at the American Educational Research Association, New York.

Merriam, S. B. (1998). *Qualitative research and case study applications in education* (2nd ed.). San Francisco, CA: Jossey-Bass Publishers.

Mertl, V. (2009). "Don't touch anything, it might break!": Adolescent musicians' accounts of collaboration and access to technologies seminal to their musical practice. In A. Dimitracopoulou, C. O'Malley, D. Suthers, & P. Reimann (Eds.), *Proceedings of the Eighth International Conference on Computer Supported Collaborative Learning (CSCL).* Rhodes, Greece: International Society of the Learning Sciences Inc.

Mertl, V., O'Mahony, K., Honwad, S., Tyson, K., Herrenkohl, L. R., & Hoadley, C. (2008). Analyzing collaborative contexts: Professional musicians, corporate engineers, and communities in the Himalayas. In S. A. Barab, K. E. Hay, & D. T. Hickey (Eds.), *Proceedings of the Ninth International Conference of the Learning Sciences (ICLS). Utrecht, The Netherlands.* Mahwah, NJ: Lawrence Erlbaum.

Mertl, V., & Herrenkohl, L. R. (2006). *Dispositions: Bridging the intellectual, social, and personal dimension of learning.* Paper presented at the American Educational Research Association, San Francisco, CA.

Michaels, S., Shouse, A. W., & Schweingruber, H. A. (2008). *Ready, set, science! Putting research to work in k-8 science classrooms. Board on science education, center for education, division of behavioral and social sciences and education.* Washington, DC: The National Academies Press.

Moll, L. C. (1990). Introduction. In L. C. Moll (Ed.), *Vygotsky and education: Instructional implications and applications of sociohistorical psychology* (pp. 1–27). New York, NY: Cambridge University Press.

Moll, L. C. (2001). Through the mediation of others: Vygotskian research on teaching. In V. Richardson (Ed.), *Handbook of research on teaching* (4th ed., pp. 111–129). Washington, DC: AERA Wittrock, M.C.

Moll, L. C., & Greenberg, J. B. (1990). Creating zones of possibilities: Combining socialcontexts for instruction. In L. C. Moll (Ed.), *Vygotsky and education:*

Instructional implications and applications of sociohistorical psychology (pp. 319–348). New York, NY: Cambridge University Press.

Nasir, N. S. (2006). *But when is identity?: Challenges and tensions in operationalizing identity in studies of learning.* Unpublished manuscript.

Nasir, N. S., & Hand, V. M. (2006). Exploring sociocultural perspectives on race, culture, and learning. *Review of Educational Research, 76(4),* 449–479.

Nasir, N.S., Rosebery, A.S., Warren, B., and Lee, C.D. (2006). Learning as a cultural process. In R. K. Sawyer (Ed.), *The Cambridge Handbook of the Learning Sciences* (pp. 489–504). New York, NY: Cambridge University Press.

National Research Council. (2007). *Taking science to school: Learning and teaching science in grades K-8.* Washington, DC: The National Academies Press.

National Research Council. (2009). *Learning science in informal environments: People, places, and pursuits.* Washington, DC: The National Academies Press.

Nussbaum, M. (1997). *Cultivating humanity: A classical defense of reform in liberal education.* Cambridge: Harvard University Press.

Nussbaum, M. (1999). The discernment of perception: An Aristotelian conception of private and public rationality. In N. Sherman (Ed.), *Aristotle's ethics* (pp. 145–181). Lanham: Rowman and Littlefield.

O'Connor, K. (2001). Contextualization and the negotiation of social identities in a situated learning project. *Linguistics & Education, 12(3),* 285–308.

O'Connor, K. (2003). Communicative practice, cultural production, and situated learning: Constructing and contesting identities of expertise in a heterogeneous learning context. In S. Wortham & B. Rymes (Eds.), *The linguistic anthropology of education.* Westport, CT: Praeger.

O'Connor, M. C., & Michaels, S. (1993). Aligning academic task and participation status through revoicing: analysis of a classroom discourse strategy. *Anthropology and Education Quarterly, 24(4),* 318–335.

O'Connor, M. C., & Michaels, S. (1996). Shifting participant frameworks: orchestrating thinking practices in group discussion. In D. Hicks (Ed.), *Child discourse and social learning* (pp. 63–102). Cambridge: Cambridge University Press.

Oatley, K., & Nundy, S. (1996). Rethinking the role of emotions in education. In D. R. Olson & N. Torrance (Eds.), *The handbook of education and human development: New models of learning, teaching, and schooling* (pp. 257–274). Oxford, UK: Blackwell.

Ochs, E., Schieffelin, B., & Platt, M., " in, ed. by.. (1979). Propositions across utterances and speakers. In E. Ochs & B. Schieffelin (Eds.), *Developmental pragmatics* (pp. 251–268). New York, NY: Academic Press.

Packer, M. J., & Goicoechea, J. (2000). Sociocultural and constructivist theories of learning: Ontology, not just epistemology. *Educational Psychologist, 35(4),* 227–241.

Palincsar, A. S., & Brown, A. L. (1984). Reciprocal teaching of comprehension-fostering and comprehension-monitoring activities. *Cognition and Instruction, 1(2),* 117–175.

Payton, J., Weissberg, R. P., Durlack, J. A., Dymnicki, A. B., Taylor, R. D., Schellinger, K. B., et al. (2008). *The positive impact of social and emotional learning for kindergarten to eighth-grade students: Findings from three scientific reviews.* Chicago, IL: Collaborative for Academic, Social, and Emotional Learning (CASEL).

Piaget, J. (1970). *Science of education and the psychology of the child* (D. Coltman, Trans.). New York, NY: Orion Press.

Polman, J. L. (2004). Dialogic activity structures for project-based learning environments. *Cognition and Instruction, 22(4)*, 431–466.

Rogoff, B. (1990). *Apprenticeship in thinking: Cognitive development in social context.* New York, NY: Oxford University Press.

Rogoff, B. (1994). Developing understanding of the idea of communities of learners. *Mind, Culture, and Activity, 1(4)*, 209–229.

Rogoff, B. (1995). Observing sociocultural activity on three planes: participatory appropriation, guided participation, and apprenticeship. In J.V. Wertsch, P. D. Rio, & A. Alvarez (Eds.), *Sociocultural studies of mind* (pp. 139–164). Cambridge: Cambridge University Press.

Rogoff, B. (2003). *The cultural nature of human development.* New York, NY: Oxford University Press.

Rose, M. (1995). *Possible lives: The promise of public education in America.* Boston, MA: Houghton Mifflin.

Rosebery, A. S., & Warren, B. (2000). *Children's ways with words in science and mathematics: A conversation across disciplines.* Madison, WI: University of Wisconsin-Madison.

Rosebery, A. S., & Warren, B. (2008). Introduction. In A. S. Rosebery & B. Warren (Eds.), *Teaching science to English language learners: Building on students' strengths.* Arlington, VA: National Science Teachers Association.

Rosebery, A. S., Warren, B., & Conant, F. R. (1992). Appropriating scientific discourse: Findings from language minority classrooms. *Journal of Learning Sciences, 2(1)*, 61–94.

Rutherford, F. J., & Ahlgren, A. (1990). *Science for all Americans, American Association for the Advancement of Science.* New York, NY: Oxford University Press.

Sawyer, R. K. (2006). *The Cambridge handbook of the learning sciences.* New York, NY: Cambridge University Press.

Schauble, L. (1990). Belief revision in children: The role of prior knowledge and strategies for generating evidence. *Journal of Experimental Child Psychology, 49*, 31–57.

Schauble, L., Klopfer, L., & Raghavan, K. (1991). Students' transformation from an engineering model to a science model of experimentation. *Journal of Research in Science Teaching, 28(9)*, 859–882.

Shulman, L. S., & Quinlan, K. M. (1996). The comparative psychology of school subjects. In D. Berliner & R. Calfee (Eds.), *Handbook of educational psychology* (pp. 399–673). New York, NY: Simon & Schuster Macmillan.

Siegler, R. S. (1985). Encoding and the development of problem solving. In S. F. Chipman, W. Segal & R. Glaser (Eds.), *Thinking and learning skills.* Mahwah, NJ: Lawrence Erlbaum.

Sinclair, J. M., & Coulthard, R. M. (1975). *Toward and analysis of discourse: The English used by teachers and pupils.* Oxford: Oxford University Press.

Songer, N. B., & Linn, M. C. (1991). How do students' views of science influence knowledge integration? *Journal of Research in Science Teaching, 28(761–784)*.

Spiro, M. E. (1982). Collective representations and mental representations in religious symbol systems. In J. Maquet (Ed.), *On symbols in anthropology: Essays in honor of Harry Hoijer* (pp. 45–72). Malibu: Udena Publications.

Stevens, R., O'Connor, K., & Garrison, L. (2005). *Engineering student identities in the navigation of the undergraduate curriculum.* Paper presented at the American Society for Engineering Education Annual Conference & Exposition.

Stigler, J. W., & Hiebert, J. (1998). Teaching is a cultural activity. *American Educator*, 22(4), 4–11.

Tharp, R. G., & Gallimore, R. (1988). *Rousing minds to life: Teaching, learning, and schooling in social context.* New York, NY: Cambridge University Press.

Tomasello, M. (1999). *The cultural origins of human cognition.* Cambridge, MA: Harvard University Press.

Toulmin, S. (1992). *Cosmopolis: The hidden agenda of modernity.* Chicago, IL: University of Chicago Press.

Veer, R., Van der. (2001). The idea of units of analysis: Vygotsky's contribution. In S. Chaiklin (Ed.), *The theory and practice of cultural-historical pedagogy* (pp. 93–106). Aarhus, DK: Aarhus University Press.

Veer, R., Van der. (2007). Vygotsky in context: 1900–1935. In H. Daniels, M. Cole & J. V. Wertsch (Eds.), *The Cambridge companion to Vygotsky* (pp. 21–50). New York, NY: Cambridge University Press.

Veer, R., Van der, & Valsiner, J. (1991). *Understanding Vygotsky: A quest for synthesis.* Oxford, England: Blackwell.

Veresov, N. (1999). *Undiscovering Vygotsky: Etudes on the prehistory of cultural-historical psychology.* Frankfurt am Main, Germany: Peter Lang.

Vygotsky, L. S. (1978). *Mind in society: The development of higher psychological processes.* Cambridge, MA: Harvard University Press.

Vygotsky, L. S. (1987/1934). Thinking and speech (N. Minick, Trans.). In R. W. Rieber & A. S. Carton (Eds.), *The collected works of L.S. Vygotsky* (Vol. 1). New York, NY: Plenum Press.

Wahl, K. H., & Blackhurst, A. (2000). Factors affecting the occupational and educational aspirations of children and adolescents. *Professional School Counseling*, 3(5), 367–374.

Warren, B., Ballenger, C., Ogonowski, M., Rosebery, A. S., & Hudicourt-Barnes, J. (2001). Rethinking diversity in learning science: The logic of everyday sensemaking. *Journal of Research in Science Teaching*, 38(5), 529–552.

Warren, B., Rosebery, A. S., & Conant, F. R. (1989). *Cherche konnen: science and literacy in language minority classrooms* (No. 7305). Cambridge, MA: Bolt, Beranek & Newman.

Wenger, E. (1998). *Communities of practice: Learning, meaning, and identity.* New York, NY: Cambridge University Press.

Wertsch, J. V. (1988). *Vygotsky and the social formation of mind.* Cambridge, MA: Harvard University Press.

Wertsch, J. V. (1991). *Voices of the mind: A sociocultural approach to mediated action.* Cambridge, MA: Harvard University Press.

Wertsch, J. V. (1998). *Mind as action.* New York, NY: Oxford University Press.

Wertsch, J. V., & Rupert, L. J. (1993). The authority of cultural tools in a sociocultural approach to mediated agency. *Cognition and Instruction*, 11, 227–240.

Windschitl, M., Thompson, J., & Braaten, M. (in press). Beyond the scientific method: Model-based inquiry as a new paradigm of preference for school science investigations. *Science Education*.

Wineburg, S., & Grossman, P. (2001). Affect and effect in cognitive approaches to instruction. In S. Carver & D. Klahr (Eds.), *Cognition and instruction: Twenty-five years of progress* (pp. 475–488). Mahwah, NJ: Lawrence Erlbaum.

Wortham, S. (2004). The interdependence of social identification and learning. *American Educational Research Journal*, 41, 715–750.

Wortham, S. (2006). *Learning identity: The joint emergence of social identification and academic learning*. New York, NY: Cambridge University Press.

Yackel, E., & Cobb, P. (1996). Sociomathematical norms, argumentation, and autonomy in mathematics. *Journal for Research in Mathematics Education*, 27, 458–477.

Yamakawa, Y., Forman, E., & Ansell, E. (2009). Role of positioning: The role of positioning in constructing an identity in a third grade mathematics classroom. In K. Kumpulainen, C. E. Hmelo-Silver & M. César (Eds.), *Investigating classroom interaction: Methodologies in action* (pp. 179–202). Rotterdam: Sense Publishers.

Index

(*Continued from page iii*)

Computation and Human Experience
Philip E. Agre

Situated Cognition: On Human Knowledge and Computer Representations
William J. Clancey

Communities of Practice: Learning, Meaning, and Identity
Etienne Wenger

Learning in Likely Places: Varieties of Apprenticeship in Japan
John Singleton, Editor

Talking Mathematics in School: Studies of Teaching and Learning
Magdalene Lampert and Merrie L. Blunk, Editors

Perspectives on Activity Theory
Yrjö Engeström, Reijo Miettinen, and Raija-Leena Punamäki, Editors

Dialogic Inquiry: Towards a Socio-cultural Practice and Theory of Education
Gordon Wells

Vygotskian Perspectives on Literacy Research: Constructing Meaning Through Collaborative Inquiry
Carol D. Lee and Peter Smagorinsky, Editors

Technology in Action
Christian Heath and Paul Luff

Changing Classes: School Reform and the New Economy
Martin Packer

Building Virtual Communities: Learning and Change in Cyberspace
K. Ann Renninger and Wesley Shumar, Editors

Adult Learning and Technology in Working-Class Life
Peter Sawchuk

Vygotsky's Educational Theory in Cultural Context
Alex Kozulin, Boris Gindis, Vladimir S. Ageyev, and Suzanne M. Miller, Editors

The Learning in Doing series was founded in 1987
by Roy Pea and John Seely Brown.